# Being Virtual

# Being Virtual

## Who You Really Are Online

Davey Winder

Copyright © 2008    Davey Winder

Published by    John Wiley & Sons Ltd, The Atrium, Southern Gate, Chichester,
West Sussex PO19 8SQ, England

Telephone (+44) 1243 779777

Email (for orders and customer service enquiries): cs-books@wiley.co.uk
Visit our Home Page on www.wileyeurope.com or www.wiley.com

**Other Wiley Editorial Offices**

John Wiley & Sons Inc., 111 River Street, Hoboken, NJ 07030, USA

Jossey-Bass, 989 Market Street, San Francisco, CA 94103-1741, USA

Wiley-VCH Verlag GmbH, Boschstr. 12, D-69469 Weinheim, Germany

John Wiley & Sons Australia Ltd, 42 McDougall Street, Milton, Queensland 4064, Australia

John Wiley & Sons (Asia) Pte Ltd, 2 Clementi Loop #02-01, Jin Xing Distripark, Singapore 129809

John Wiley & Sons Ltd, 6045 Freemont Blvd, Mississauga, Ontario L5R 4J3, Canada

Wiley also publishes its books in a variety of electronic formats. Some content that appears in print may not be available in electronic books.

**British Library Cataloguing in Publication Data**

A catalogue record for this book is available from the British Library

ISBN 978-0-470-72362-3

Typeset in 9.5 on 14 pt SM DIN by SNP Best-set Typesetter Ltd., Hong Kong
Printed and bound by Printer Trento in Italy

To Dad, the greatest man I ever knew. How I wish I could tell you that . . .

# Acknowledgements

**A few of the very many people** who helped make this possible:

Cia Bergholm, Sally Berry, Richard Botley, Steve Cassidy, Greg Chute, Graham Cluley, Jennifer Conway, Simon Cooke, Anna Crawford, Sarah Crawford, 'Daisy', Nathan and Kelly Davalos, Sarah Gavin, Alicia Gonzales, Simon Jones, Alistair Kelman, Rosie Kemp, Andrew Kennerley, Sara Landymore, Jeff Laschuk, Rhonda Lillie, Mark A. Moctezuma, Brian and Laurie Pearson, Howard Rheingold, Taina Rodriguez, Ron76, Graham Sadd, Vincent Scheurer, Buddy Schreiber, Catherine Smith, Simon Stevens, Malin Ströman, Sarah Thomas, Michael Wilson, Yvonne Winder and all the avatars I encountered along the way . . .

# Contents

# Preface: New Beginnings

**Thanks to the Internet, it** has never been so easy to become the person of your wildest dreams.

Immersive 3D worlds such as Second Life and There.com have provided an escape route from the ordinary, places where the extraordinary is commonplace. Forget about walking, wheelchair users can fly. Balding, middle-aged men with beer bellies and bad breath transform into the slim Lothario of their darkest fantasies. Pensioners wipe away the pains of age, rediscovering youthful exuberance and making young friends once more. Race is no longer important in a world where orange aliens are the norm. Gender is determined not by X and Y chromosomes but bits and bytes alone. In the virtual world you have the chance to impact upon and nurture the very real lives of others regardless of race, culture, class or location. Perhaps, more importantly, in the virtual world you have the divine power to create life, your life, and mould it into pretty much anything you please.

In the **virtual** world you have the **divine power** to create life, **your** life, and mould it into **pretty much anything you please**

In the real world we rely heavily upon knowing the identity, or at least something about it, of the people we communicate with. Without this knowledge we have difficulty in being able to truly understand the interactions we have. Online there are no clues to identity beyond the masks we choose to wear, figuratively when it comes to text-based conversations and literally within emerging 3D virtual worlds.

No wonder it has become harder than ever to honestly answer the question: who am I?

We place a heavy emphasis on the physical attributes of the people we meet in order to determine a précis of their identity. Ever judged a book by its cover? So can we possibly hope to cope in the online world where these visual clues are as fantastical as their creator fancies? Is dressing up in the pixel fabric of an avatar skin really any less of a premeditated disguise than whatever we happen to pick from the wardrobe today?

**The author as seen by There.com users.**

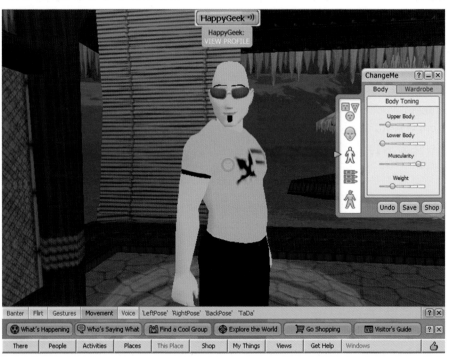

> Avatar: the original Sanskrit word means the descent of a deity from heaven, and is used in Hinduism to refer to the earthly incarnation of that deity. However, within the online realm of virtual reality, an avatar is the digital representation you choose to portray yourself on screen.

Sartre famously insisted that 'I am my body to the extent that I am', but today he might be forced into changing his mind. After all, with multiple bodies in the form of in-world avatars, does this mean that we must have multiple identities to match? Although we are certainly free to create as many personalities online as time and patience allow, we can still only possess one true identity.

Think of personality as being the sum of its parts: behavioural, temperamental, emotional and mental. One's personality can change from day to day or month to month, whereas an identity is the distinct personality that remains as a persisting entity. It is the individual characteristics that enable you to be recognised apart from everyone else. Most of the time we are not creating a real personality let alone an identity online, but rather what Jung would call a persona, a personal façade to be presented to the world.

Now ask yourself the question: who do I become when I log in, and who do I leave behind when logging out?

It's a question I have been attempting to answer ever since 1989.

This was the year that:

- George Bush replaced Ronald Reagan as the forty-first President of the USA and within a year had declared war (like father, like son perhaps).

- Sky TV was launched in Europe (and slowly started to change the technology, and the face, of television forever).
- Margaret Thatcher introduced the poll tax (and a resurgence of direct action as a direct result).
- Nintendo launched the Game Boy (paving the way for ever more portable games machines).
- The Tiananmen Square massacre took hundreds of lives (and changed nothing).

And the writer formerly known as David William Winder died.

# I had the mortgage, the cars, the Filofax and absolutely no sense of belonging to anything

I went from a good job in sports management, involved in the running of golf and snooker clubs in Surrey, to managing one of the largest used Ford car franchises in the country. My identity was certainly never in doubt: I was your archetypal career man. Working hard to provide for my young family, I also played as hard as any young man with money would. I had the mortgage, the cars, the Filofax and absolutely no sense of belonging to anything.

That was early in 1989, before the fateful night later that same year when I contracted viral encephalitis. Thankfully, a rare disease, related to meningitis, encephalitis destroyed a ridiculous number of brain cells and left me in hospital for the worst part of a year. Emerging from my deep sleep, I awoke in the Atkinson Morley specialist neurological hospital paralysed in both legs and one arm, clouded in confusion and unable to bear the smallest amount of light upon my eyes. I also suffered from a mercifully mild dysphasia whereby I was unable to communicate properly verbally. This is best described as having a box full of words and being unable to find the right ones to finish a monkey. So much of what I had to say was almost surreal in its quality, just like that last sentence. You might think that things could only get better from this point on.

Then the blood clots arrived.

They travelled up from my legs and into my lungs. At least I was in the right place during the next couple of weeks, during which time I endured half a dozen of these pulmonary emboli. I didn't actually die for longer than a few seconds in that hospital, but I did die deep inside myself.

My wife stood by me, often literally, during those long and painful months in hospital. She provided the comfort and support that was crucial to my survival, a link to my life outside that place, a link to my family. She even stood by me once I was discharged early in 1990, helping with the transition from institutionalised familiarity into the very unfamiliar world I found myself deposited in.

Not only had I lost my job during this period of illness, but my house was soon to follow. This was not altogether a bad thing as I am not sure how long I could have lived, if that is the right word, unable to leave the sofa other than to be wheeled into the hallway to use a bedpan or bottle. At least once the house was repossessed I found myself in a specially adapted ground floor flat. Comfortable in that vaguely medical sense, with winch over the bath and ramp into the garden, and being part of a council sheltered-accommodation scheme for the elderly added nicely to the care-home ambience.

For a few months Joanne continued to look after the man she had fallen in love with and the father of her two very young children. Yet it soon became apparent that she was looking after someone else entirely. The encephalitis had changed me far more than my physical appearance alone suggested. My mood swings were ferocious, my depression as deep and dark as they come.

To appreciate just how rough the mental terrain was, when I left hospital I was unable to read or write and had the concentration span of a goldfish. My sense of spatial awareness had also been severely compromised, partly due to the fortunately temporary inflammation of my optic nerves, which left me photophobic and with tunnel vision, and partly due to the brain damage which left me totally unaware of the left-hand side of everything. Imagine trying to tell the time if your perception of a clock face is a right hand semicircle with the numbers 1 to 12 arranged around its edge. I was most certainly not the man Joanne had married a few short years before. Truth be told, David William Winder had died sometime during the preceding year.

I cannot be sure exactly when 'I' became 'IT'. Maybe it was the moment when the virus first struck and destroyed a swathe of brain cells leaving me confused and weak. Maybe it was later as the infection spread and the paralysis set in. One thing I know for sure is that the useless man who found himself trapped inside a useless body without the safety net of a fully functioning mind was not 'ME'.

The trouble is I no longer knew who 'me' was, nor would I for many years to come. My search for identity would take me on a long and truly amazing journey through a world that had no place in reality. A world that existed only in the bits and bytes of a computer network and the bits and pieces of my shattered mind.

As I searched for myself, my wife searched for and found someone else. She went from living with a stranger to starting afresh with another stranger. I do not blame her now; who knows how I would have reacted had the shoe been on the other foot?

At the time my anger and sadness combined within a truly broken man. My wife and kids were gone, and I was left alone apart from a home help to clean the house and householder alike, and a computer. When it came to identity I had none, I was a blank canvas waiting for the portrait of my personality to be painted upon it. But first I needed to rediscover some basic survival skills, I needed to learn to read and write again for a start. My late father taught me, using a combination of Janet and John books together with an incredible display of patience. It could not have been easy seeing your grown-up son struggling with 'the cat sat on the mat'. An Amstrad PCW word processor with delusions of computing grandeur was pressed into service and slowly taught me to write courtesy of a basic spellchecker.

## When it **came** to **identity** I had **none,** I was a **blank** canvas waiting for the **portrait of my personality** to be **painted** upon **it**

Repetition proved to be the key as far as the miracle organ that is the brain is concerned. This 1.5 kilograms of electrical impulses that controls every aspect of our existence from the physical to the psychological is clever enough to reconnect pathways, powering up new processes to take over control from those damaged parts.

The cleverly adapted flat was all well and good, but in the early days I could not venture outside without someone to push the National Health Service wheelchair. Things didn't improve much when I progressed to a truly humongous electric wheelchair which provided the illusion of being able to move under my own steam. An illusion that was soon shattered when the shackles of battery life became apparent. Not that I could get that far on my own; kerbs and cars parked on pavements conspired against me in that regard.

I was, in spite of everything, stuck in a small flat with just my own sorry arse for company most of the day. Nights were for medication-induced sleeping, as a social life for cripples had apparently not been invented at this stage. It is amazing how quickly you discover who your true friends are when your money and your health have gone. I discovered that I had none at all. What I did have was a modem the size of a shoebox which connected to my telephone handset by way of rubber suction cups and which transferred data about as quickly as a tortoise wearing flippers and swimming through porridge. The technology was primitive, but so was my urge to communicate. Getting online wasn't easy, nor cheap, but it was all I had. It was my only chance to find out who I was . . .

Within the pages of this book you will encounter many people for whom the online world has been a voyage of discovery.

- Buddy is severely disabled by cerebral palsy, but in the virtual world can override patronising stereotypes while making friends in the real world who have agreed to assume his care should anything happen to his mother.
- Daisy has found the freedom to express her sexuality online, whereas memories of childhood abuse prevents her from doing the same in real life.
- Mark has built a new virtual life and career online which flourishes as his real one continues to crumble financially and emotionally.
- Ronnie fell in love **and** got married in a virtual world, eventually splitting up with his wife before they ever met for real.
- Sarah discovered a feeling of belonging online, missing in the real world, that helped shape her teenage years.
- Sally, a 68-year-old website owner, has found an environment where older people are represented by their actions and not their grey hair.
- Brian not only adopts a female gender in the virtual world, but entered into a virtual lesbian relationship which developed into a real-life heterosexual affair.

- Jeff runs a virtual business selling virtual clothing to avatars in the virtual world, and makes enough money to pay his real-life bills.
- Richard discovered a dark side of himself through the medium of multiplayer online games, a dark side that led to him becoming addicted to murder.
- Simon lived out his fantasy of being a rock star during an elaborate virtual hoax that lasted many years.

If the face is the index of the mind, then surely the Internet has become the mirror to the soul . . .

**Who is the real Davey Winder?**

# Foreword

**It is said that in 1984**, with his book *Neuromancer*, William Gibson "created" the genre of "cyberpunk" science fiction, and with it, the concept of "cyberspace" as an alternate reality for protagonists to live out their lives in, on a part or full-time basis, as the author preferred.

In 1992, Neal Stephenson (*Snow Crash*) took it a step further, and made these virtual realities part of almost everyone's lives, becoming the venue for everything from pizza deliveries to relationships to high crimes and international intrigue.

By 1994, Melissa Scott (*Trouble and Her Friends*) and others had made cyberspace a mainstay for science fiction authors and an acceptable setting for all kinds of stories and plot lines.

At the same time, technology was rushing ahead at an equally breakneck pace, and the concept of cyberspace along with it. However, unlike fictional cyberspace, the transition of human activity onto the real Internet has been far from neat or clearly defined.

Some will tell you that the transition started with the first email message which captured the sender's thoughts and delivered them, albeit in something quite less than "3D" to the receiver.

Others will tell you that it began with the Access-80 BBS in 1977, which was arguably the first bulletin board system to allow multiple people to be "on line" at the same time.

And Richard Bartle will tell you that *he* started it all in 1979 when he invented the MUD, or "multi-user dungeon" environment on Essex Universities' DEC-10 mini computer.

Since we will ultimately find that the real story of cyberspace is the story of the people in it, I choose to accept Dr. Bartle's claim, since a dungeon is a far more interesting place for a story than a dreary corporate email, sort of the modern equivalent of Alexander Graham Bell's "Watson, come here, I need you".

Graphical "cyberspace" first made its appearance in 1987 as a multiplayer flight simulator, and quickly evolved as game developers recognized the multiuser environment as an important form of gameplay, and, therefore revenue. Cyberspace became defined as "Massively Multiplayer Online" (MMO) environments, where anywhere from scores to thousands of players participated as knights, trolls, villains, heroes, giant sentient cows, you name it. Games like Ultima Online and World of Warcraft have gone from being the exclusive domain of socially deficient teenage boys to "The New Golf" for people of all ages and genders.

But, unlike Gibson and Stephenson's Cyberspace, who you are in these environments is ultimately determined by the game's authors – the so-called Game Gods – not you. Sure, you can choose if you're going to be a hunter or a warrior, an elf or a cow, but in the end, it's the game that gives you those choices, not you. And unlike Cyberspace, these environments have a built-in goal, usually associated with puzzle solving, exploring, or defeating opponents of some sort, all of which are carefully crafted to provide you hours of entertainment.

In the late 1990s, some people began to think of cyberspace or MMOs as *extensions* of people's lives, and not *replacements* for them. Instead of shedding your day-to-day persona as, say, a high-powered music executive to become, for example, a 2-foot 4-inch elf hunter with a sideline as a leatherworker, you would instead use the MMO to appear as something resembling a real person for the purpose of meeting and communicating with other people.

To some this might have seemed to be a radical idea, but it actually was a completely unsurprising step (in retrospect) in the evolution of the Web. From the advent of the first email, or first MUD character if you prefer, people have been using technology to communicate more immediately and effectively – through bulletin text-based environments like IRC (Internet relay chat), MUDs (multi-user dungeons, domains or dimensions), bulletin boards, and instant messaging. When the Web came along, they expanded their communications and expression to include blogs, graphics, photos and videos in an explosion of self-expression which has driven sites like MySpace and YouTube to mainstream popularity.

While all of this made it easier to express yourself in more and more creative ways, they all weren't the same as "being there". The asynchronicity of blogs and MySpace pages made it easy for you to communicate, but lacked the immediacy of real interaction.

Enter social virtual worlds. In 1997, Will Harvey and Jeffery Ventrella got the idea of a MMO environment as a "place" for people to meet, socialize and create, as opposed to just being participants in a pre-set agenda. Their ideas, along with the help of many others, became There.com, the first truly social virtual world. Others, such as Second Life, quickly followed, creating a whole new category of online activity.

Like all new technologies, There and other social virtual worlds were at first limited by technology, and then by their obscurity as technological oddities. That all changed in 2005, when graphics in commodity personal computers brought products like There (and World of Warcraft, incidentally) within reach of Mom and Dad's personal computer. What some view as the true tipping point into popular culture occurred in 2006, when MTV launched Virtual Laguna Beach, a virtual world built on top of There's technology, and the most popular discourse in virtual worlds went from discussions of BIOS levels and video cards to phrases like "Do you have a boyfriend in here?".

As they emerged from obscurity into the mainstream, virtual worlds became the subject of many articles, books, documentaries, and episodes of popular TV shows. Until now, all have focused on the worlds themselves, their technology, the companies who run them, or a few select individuals doing "extraordinary" things (if you can call making a million un-real dollars selling un-real land "extraordinary").

Social virtual worlds shifted the balance of power in these cyberspaces from the Game Gods to the participants, who were using this technology as an extension of their lives and as a new way to engage with others, on their own terms. And "their own terms" often meant engaging with the virtual world in ways very different from how they engaged in the real world.

*Being Virtual* is the first book to focus on the *real* content of virtual worlds: the people who inhabit them and their stories. Because no matter how different you may be from your "avatar", it is you who invented it, and it is in some way reflective of *who* you are. *Being Virtual* brings you the back story behind the characters, and helps us begin to understand the true impact of these environments on today's society, and, interestingly enough, vice versa.

As these environments become more and more commonplace, understanding how they fit into our lives becomes more important, whether we use them to communicate, or whether we know other people who do so. As a part of the fabric of our day-to-day lives, like email, instant and text messaging, understanding the real people in the environments is as important as understanding the environments themselves.

Michael Wilson, CEO, There.com

# I Identity Crisis

**What does identity mean in this** increasingly connected and uncompromisingly digital world?

Behind every avatar there is a real person, but why do we adopt the virtual personalities that we do and how can the choices that we make in the virtual world impact our real lives and the lives of those with whom we interact both online and off?

By looking at the virtual world through the eyes of its inhabitants, listening to their tales of mind-boggling gender-bending love triangles and heart-warming escapes from the bondage of disability, it is possible to find out.

**The Second Life version of the author.**

# Online Tribes

**In 1973 the BBC launched** a radio programme called *Does He Take Sugar?* This gave disabled people a voice in the media, a chance to shout 'I am more than my disability' to anyone who was listening. Fast-forward to my dingy council flat on the warden-controlled sheltered-accommodation estate, and you would have found that nothing had actually changed in the 17 years since. I was, in real life, victim to the 'does he take sugar' syndrome every day of my life. Most people would speak to anyone who happened to be with me, as if I wasn't there at all. Any-thing than risk patronisingly fleeting eye contact, shrouded in a cloak of caring concern, with the obviously retarded man in the huge electric wheelchair. Not that they could see my eyes behind the dark glasses I was forced to wear for fear of the light that would burn into them like red-hot needles of fire.

I guess I cannot blame them, I was hard to look at: imagine Hell's Angel crossed with Vietnam War veteran. The long beard, the hand strapped into a splint to prevent it from forming the claw it tried so hard to be, the permanently angry expression and ill-mannered demeanour. No wonder most people did not try to speak directly to me, no wonder they opted for the safety of speaking to someone else or walking on by.

Yet online there was no escape option. There was no carer standing by to deflect attention away from the highly vocal individual who had a habit of saying the most inappropriate things at the most inappropriate of times. Call it disability-induced Tourette's syndrome if you like. Heck, call it anything you want, but when you are constantly being ignored you will try anything to grab a small piece of attention.

Any parent will recognise this pattern of behaviour. In fact there is no doubt that those who encountered me in my first few months online would have assumed I was a kid, that the bulletin board systems of cyberspace were my playground. With my tendency to be overdramatic, bawdy and unpredictable that was not an alto-gether erroneous assumption.

As far as my identity and personality were concerned I **was** immature. The fact that this was a 25-year-old man who had been working his way up the management ladder just a couple of years before was neither here nor there: that person was gone, that personality had been retired to the deepest, darkest corners of my cerebral cortex.

That personality was **not** coming back; my inner child would not allow it.

Yes, I was a developing child and cyberspace was my playground. A very public playground as it happens: a very public place to make one's mistakes, to bare ones' self emotionally and to discover who you really are.

## FidoNet

A network of bulletin board systems, primarily using the same 'Fido' software, that was hugely popular in the early 1990s, before the World Wide Web came along. FidoNet (www.fidonet.org) still exists today but is a mere shadow of its former self.

My first taste of online life was on one of the many FidoNet bulletin board systems that had sprung up across Europe and North America at the very end of the 1980s.

## Bulletin Board System

A Bulletin Board System (BBS) was simply a computer running software that allowed people to connect to it via the telephone and a modem. Hugely popular throughout the 1980s and early 1990s, BBSs were a social phenomenon where people met to exchange software and ideas alike.

These hobbyist systems allowed anyone with a modem and telephone to connect, but only one at a time, because the BBS itself was contained within a computer hanging off a single telephone line, more often than not in the owner's bedroom. Once connected you could read messages within subject-specific categories, and reply in a linear fashion. Thus online conversations were constructed, and friendships made. It was possible to use software to download all the messages in a couple of minutes, and then hang up the line. Not only did this free up the BBS so that more people could participate, but it kept the costs down. Once you had replied to postings, the off-line reader would reconnect and post them for you, downloading the next set of unread messages at the same time allowing the communication cycle to continue.

I journeyed through other systems, very primitive virtual worlds where the landscape was created by nothing more than text on a screen yet where I felt accepted more than in any wretched concrete habitat populated by total strangers. Already

I felt like I had found a new place to live, but I had yet to find a new home or my new identity. That would have to wait for another death, the demise of a popular online bulletin board called Micronet800.

I had stumbled across this British Telecom-owned service, part of the Post Office Prestel system which is best described as TeleText over the telephone. As bizarre as the concept sounds today, back in the late 1980s the idea of a non-scrolling, blocky $40 \times 24$ text character window with the most primitive 'graphics' imaginable was actually quite revolutionary stuff. If you want to know what it looks like, pop into a high street travel agent, as many still use a very similar Viewdata system for making bookings to this day.

Even the price wasn't enough to put people off, which was in itself quite an achievement when you consider you had to pay for the cost of the telephone call by the minute, a monthly subscription fee for Prestel access and then anything up to 99p for every single screen of information you looked at. Micronet800 was the killer application for me though, so called because it was accessed via page *800# on Prestel. This online magazine not only provided its readers with computer related articles and gossip, but also access to many pioneering services that are now taken for granted by users of the Internet, such as online games (StarNet was a kind of text-driven online chess game that got updated once every day as combatants attempted to rule the universe) and chat rooms.

Unsurprisingly, I found myself strangely drawn to the latter.

Nothing like the chat rooms of today, these were limited by the frame-based operation at Prestel, which meant that messages scrolled off the screen never to appear again if you did not read them quickly enough. This made conversation a difficult process on occasion, and led to many a surreal exchange of words. Conversation was also limited by moderation, with Micronet staff ensuring obscene and libellous messages were deleted as quickly as possible. Perhaps the most obvious limitation was that you could only chat between the hours of 8 and 10 p.m.!

# This was **my introduction** to the **possibility** of **identity play**, although for **me** it was **no game**

But none of this mattered because it was here that I encountered the notion of online tribalism for the first time. Micronetters were very different people from FidoNetters in their outlook, their conversations and their online personalities. How strange considering, as I came to realise soon enough, lots of people used both systems. Yet there was no denying that they exhibited wildly different online personas.

This was my introduction to the possibility of identity play, although for me it was no game. I was still a child exploring the possibilities of my persona, pushing the boundaries of the medium as well as the patience of the people who lived within it.

I had hardly had a chance to start this process of personal development when my participation at Micronet was cut short, courtesy of the system being closed down in 1991. It turned out to be a blessing in disguise, like finding your house has been demolished but the council have built you a bigger, better one in an even friendlier neighbourhood. That neighbourhood was a newly emerging online system that had agreed to take on the exiting Micronet users.

That system was called CIX, and it became both my online home and the birthplace of 'dwindera'.

## CIX

CIX (http://conferencing.cixonline.com) started life as a FidoNet Bulletin Board but went on to become the biggest online conferencing system in Europe, and the first company to provide commercial Internet email access in 1988. It remains a popular virtual community to this day.

CIX, or the Compulink Information eXchange to be formal about things, had evolved from a fairly typical back bedroom FidoNet Bulletin Board System started in 1983 by Frank and Sylvia Thornley. They turned this into a commercial business venture just 4 years later, pioneering the concept of conferencing systems in the UK. The Thornleys were ahead of their time, forward thinkers who had created a place where members could not only communicate across a broad spectrum of forums (or conferences in CIX-speak) covering every topic imaginable, but where they could actually create those conferences themselves and control who had right of access.

This ability to communicate, participate and moderate opened up new doors through which my over eager personality could, and indeed did, charge like a bull in a china shop. On CIX I was, and remain to this very day, known as dwindera. There was no clever attempt at cryptic wordplay going on, nothing clever at all. In fact, quite the opposite. I had tried to open an account using the default suggestion of dwinder, managed to do something wrong which caused that account to fail, so the system came back with its very logical appending of 'a' to my name. The next 'dwinder' would have been 'dwinderb', so I guess I got off lucky, unlike the membership of CIX who soon discovered that, depending largely on the time of day and amount of alcohol and cannabis in my system, dwindera could be either polite and witty or anarchic and pitiless. I spent, on average, 18 hours a day connected to CIX. This may sound like obsessive behaviour, and there is no doubting that finding a sense of belonging can be a powerful drug, but my reasons were a lot more pragmatic than mere addiction.

This virtual environment was not just somewhere I came to play, not just a place I could chat to people without the wheelchair grabbing their attention first and dominating the conversation thereafter, not just an opportunity to meet people from outside of my own restrictive demographic. This was the **only** place I could truly experience life, freed from the physical and cultural bondage of my disability. This was where I would start to create a new virtual identity in parallel with discovering who I had become, or perhaps more accurately was becoming, in real life.

This was the only place I could **truly experience life**, freed from the **physical and cultural bondage** of my **disability**

I quickly discovered I was not alone in searching for some meaning to my life, entering into this online voyage of discovery. Not having a job to go to, and being blessed by the curse of insomnia ever since my illness struck, I would often find myself roaming cyberspace in the wee small hours. CIX, being an almost exclusively British residency at the time, was deserted at 3 a.m. Apart from one chap called Kevin Hall. It turned out that he worked a night shift as a computer programmer and IT support guy, and we would often chat to waste away the hours.

## CIXen

CIXen is the collective noun for members of CIX, and yet more evidence of the tribalism that exists online.

During one of these conversations Kevin invited me to join a very small group of CIXen in a conference called Herestoby. When you create a conference on CIX you can make it open to any member, or closed so that people have to apply for membership. Herestoby, so called after the founding member, a chap by the name of Toby, was closed **and** confidential, so only the invited few even knew it existed.

It quickly became apparent that all of the half a dozen members were damaged goods in one way or another. We all had problems in our lives, and now we had somewhere private to talk about them without fear of ridicule or judgement. It acted not only as a form of group therapy, but created a real feeling of community that just didn't seem to exist outside of this little online world we had ended up in, victims of our circumstances.

Toby was devastated when his girlfriend ran off with his best friend, yet instead of sinking into the kind of self-destructive behaviour one might expect, he was able to talk through his innermost feelings within the Herestoby group. My suicidal tendencies were worked through in a similar manner, and slowly over the course of 6 months we became the closest of friends – yet the seven of us had never met face to face, never spoken on the telephone, never broken out from the safety of an exclusively online members-only club.

That all changed when everyone agreed to meet up at my place, chosen because I had the most problems with travel for obvious reasons. Nobody knew what to expect, least of all me. Everyone was scared that meeting in person would somehow be a destructive exercise. Nothing could be further from the truth, the online relationship was so strong, we knew each other so intimately already, that it was more like a family reunion than anything.

The **online** relationship was so **strong**, **we knew each other** so **intimately** already, that it **was more like a family reunion** than **anything**

A short-lived one as it turned out, because later that year, on New Year's Eve, Kevin died in the most horrific motorcycle accident.

This served not only to bring us closer as a group of friends, but also acted as a rite of passage for the whole of CIX. It was the catalyst that turned CIX from being just a really cool place to chat and that forced us into becoming something much more. A memorial conference was established and people started leaving tributes to Kevin, to this man who, with very few exceptions, nobody had actually met. Yet these tributes were as heartfelt as any left by a grieving family, and that is what was being revealed: Kevin was family, part of the CIX family. With his death CIX the virtual community was born. . . .

# 2 Growing Up Online

**Growing up is never easy**; just ask any teenager if you are feeling particularly brave.

Adolescence can be a bitch. As well as having to deal with hormones and responsibility, there is the never-ending pressure to establish some kind of self-identity to deal with. Do you throw your lot in with the teen crowd and endure the wrath of your adult peers, or vice versa? Striking the right balance is a matter of trial and error, a lot of error if my own teenage years were any measure of normality.

Finding myself dumped right into the beginnings of the punk era just as I became a teenager, drawn to the music, the rebellion and the feeling of belonging, I was soon wearing bondage trousers and a bad attitude. While the clothes could be taken off and the attitude toned down when grandma came to call, other aspects of this identity-building exercise came with rather less flexibility.

Being searched by the police as they raided the dingy Deptford public house I frequented at the age of 13. Getting so drunk that I fell through the plate glass window of a shop front at 14. Taking so much speed at 15 that I did not slow down until I was 16. All these things come with a certain residual effect, they shaped who I was becoming, but there was no delete key to wipe away the mistakes, no option to create a new account and start totally afresh.

Online things are not the same; online things are so very different.

Teenagers can experiment with multiple personalities, gauging the reaction of others, finding what fits and what doesn't. Make a mistake and you simply start again with a totally clean slate.

## Teenagers can experiment with multiple personalities, gauging the reaction of others, finding what fits and what doesn't

Yet it is not just the possibility of deleting your life by erasing an avatar, closing an account, becoming someone else that marks out the online world as somewhere that identities can mature in relative safety. There is the small matter of peer pressure to consider. In the real world the wisdom of crowds is all too often replaced by the mentality of morons, as best exemplified by the rise in gang culture and boy bands the world over. When everyone in your peer group is scared of looking weak, afraid to step out of line and say the wrong thing in front of every-one else, it is all too easy for the mob mentality to overpower and engulf those exposed to it. Read any newspaper, pretty much anywhere in the so-called civilised world, and you will find headlines which illustrate this chav culture all too clearly.

Online it is much easier to talk openly, even within the vaguely tribal environment of a social network, a virtual world or a massively multiplayer online role-playing game (MMORPG). MMORPGs such as World of Warcraft have become the de facto home to a lost generation of teens. 'It's only a game' is not a phrase you are likely to hear coming from their lips; it goes way beyond play as most of us think of it. This is no fire-and-forget blast on the PlayStation, no hour wasted at the Monopoly board. To the MMORPG player this is as real as life gets.

To Sarah it is family of sorts.

## Massively **Multiplayer** Online **Role**-Playing **Games** such as **World of Warcraft** have become the de facto **home** to a **lost generation** of teens

I first encountered Sarah on the CIX online conferencing system; in fact I pretty much watched her grow up there. It was a strange duplicity of sorts, a mask over a mask, because the CIX account belonged to her father, Tony. While 'tthomas' might have been the public label applied to the person posting messages from that

### MMORPG

MMORPGs are where large numbers of players participate in game play and socialise within a sprawling virtual environment. Players from all over the world connect simultaneously, forming clans, factions and guilds as well as playing as individuals.

account, 'KiBe' was without doubt the personality on view. 'KiBe was a stupid name I picked from school. In a German lesson we were writing letters to fake penpals, all starting with "Liebe". Someone's writing was so bad that one of my friends said that looks more like KiBe, I'm going to call you that now. It's capital-ised because of the funny B in German that is a double s, and I really liked Terror-vision at the time and they capitalised all the consonants in their name. Terrible teenage reasons. I got on CIX around the same time, and while no one at school ever called me it again, the name stuck in that world'. Typical teenage reasons, I would say, from a typical teenage girl.

This typicality revealed itself in many ways for Sarah, who found herself amongst a small group of friends at school but not particularly popular in the overall scheme of things. Indeed, she goes as far as to suggest that these friends were responsible for controlling her happiness in many ways. 'They were my best friends, but when there were spats it would be hard to resolve them, and it was all very hormonal teenage drama. I had some friends outside of school, but they just kind of put up with me because they liked my best friend, I always felt like a hanger on, and not at all cool'.

That all changed when Sarah discovered cyberspace and arrived at CIX in 1994 at the tender age of 14, and threw herself headlong into the 'kids chat' and 'teen' forums there. 'I started to make friends with people, intelligent people that shared my love of music, of books, of films. I found that I had lots in common with them, and with so many of them it was easy to find something to talk about'.

She soon became obsessed with this gateway into a whole new virtual world of real relationships and would spend hours every night posting to all of her new friends, having stupid conversations on the most part. The kind of things you might expect teenage girls to be chatting about with each, but Sarah wasn't discussing this stuff or releasing her angst with her circle of school friends. She was baring her emotional all to complete strangers: names on a screen, text on the page. 'I allowed one of my friends to use it a bit to chat to people, but she couldn't understand why I found it so interesting and why I didn't want to go out with her so much now.' Perhaps this just helped to accelerate the inevitable and the friends drifted apart. 'We didn't have so much in common, her boyfriend and their friends were the ones that didn't like me much, I didn't miss them at all. I think it was this point that I realised that I really did like the CIX people. They had been in the most part genuine; I had seen so much falseness in real life that it was unexpected that these people would be truthful when they could quite easily have faked it'.

> **❝** I had seen so much **falseness** in real life that **it was unexpected** that these people **would be truthful** when they could **quite easily have faked** it **❞**

When Sarah finally decided it was time to meet up with the teen crowd from CIX, her new circle of friends, one of them phoned her mother beforehand to explain who he was and why it was OK for her to get in a car with a bunch of strange guys and travel to Edinburgh. Not the kind of behaviour that is recommended in order to stay safe online, I have to admit, but hugely typical of the bond of trust that can develop so quickly within the soul-bearing, emotional tinderbox that is cyberspace. Whereas it can take months of meetings in the real world to arrive at the stage where you reveal your inner self, online it can only take a minute or two.

People are almost in a rush to declare their state of being, stripping back the façade and getting to the warts and all truth. It is almost as if they are saying, 'This is me, if you still wanna chat then let's do it, otherwise f*** off and stop wasting my

**▐▌** My online **identity allowed** me to **explore more boundaries** and **test** what I **could** and **couldn't do** in social situations **▐▌**

time'. Despite the ability to disguise and deceive, the immediacy and remoteness of the media combine to genuinely promote the most direct form of communication which is truly beautiful in its naivety. 'People feel more free online, so they're a lot more open and honest, which includes being more insulting in a way that you just wouldn't do in real life', Sarah readily admits, revealing that 'When I first got online, I was ultra polite to everyone and would try really hard not to offend. As I got used to communicating in this way and I saw how the more confident people would not pull punches quite so much, I could relax and be a bit more frank. I would say that my online identity allowed me to explore more boundaries and test what I could and couldn't do in social situations'.

Life changing is a big concept to bandy about, but as far as Sarah is concerned that is precisely what CIX was in her most vulnerable and identity-shaping years. 'Being around older people all the time led to me maturing faster than a lot of my schoolmates, which was a good thing. It allowed me to become more confident, I was happier at school because it mattered less when fallings out happened, and they happened less as we got older. I actually socialised more with the school people, as it had given more confidence to be around them'. Outside of school, Sarah cared less about what those people thought, and got on a lot better with them as a result. 'I think it was because my attitude was less needy, they were no longer the only people I could interact with outside of school'. Sarah had discovered the value of community at a time when most of her contemporaries were consumed by far more selfish, typically teenage, desires.

## Facebook

Facebook (www.facebook.com) is a social networking site that connects people with friends and others who work, study and live around them. With more than 60 million members and growing fast, Facebook is one of the 10 most visited sites on the Internet.

Community has been a recurring theme in the online life of Sarah, tthomas and KiBe one and all. She remains an active member of CIX, and even worked for its user support department for a while, but has embraced the new wave of social networks and virtual worlds with equal passion now she is all grown up. Facebook naturally features within this landscape of belonging, allowing Sarah to catch up effortlessly with old friends.

'I've found out about a University reunion, which is another group of people I had lost contact with', she told me, adding that while it may not be as meaningful as CIX was in those developing years, Facebook is right up there when it comes to useful-ness. 'I went bowling last weekend because one of my friends mentioned it on Facebook and then made it into an event and invited people. It has become just another tool for organising our social lives'.

An obsessive compulsive in real life, Sarah has to check security in her house con-tinuously and gets quite panicky when leaving for any reason. Not that you would guess from her online persona in the community that has, ironically, become something of an obsession in recent years. In World of Warcraft, Sarah mainly plays a Paladin character, Rosmarus, a champion knight for a raiding guild in the game.

## World of Warcraft

The World of Warcraft (www.worldofwarcraft.com) is the biggest MMORPG on the planet, launched in November 2004 it now has 9 million players worldwide. Its popularity amongst teens being demonstrated by an episode of the *South Park* cartoon dedicated entirely to it 'Make Love, Not Warcraft.'

**Obsessive compulsive Sarah becomes the Paladin Rosmarus when she enters the World of Warcraft.**

What many people might regard as games for geeks, the role-playing genre has for years suffered the ignominy of being associated with Billy No-Mates types fantasising about being something they are not and never will be. Yet Sarah argues that it is the same sense of community that she first discovered on CIX and later in other virtual places, that is the main appeal of signing up with a guild.

The players regard themselves as guild members first and foremost, with an almost tribal sense of belonging. They chat every night; they help each other out in-world and in real life. This is as close to a virtual family as you are ever likely to get. It's also part of the never ending process of personal development and growth as far as Sarah is concerned. 'Recently, I have felt myself more confident in real life, leading and instructing, because that is one of my roles in the Guild – having to guide people in the healing of raids'.

'I think this is something that is really going to help me at work where following promotion I will have to instruct people on what to do and when to do it. Telling people what their tasks and objectives are and the best way of doing that in the guild will be invaluable'. But you don't often have to slaughter innocents at work in order to steal their gold, at least not literally. A raiding guild, as the name suggests, exists within the game world to steal what others have created. 'I don't particularly adopt dark roles in these games, I don't gank people unnecessarily', Sarah insists.

## Ganking

Ganking is a term that has sprung up within World of Warcraft to refer to when a group of people kill a single opponent; it is the abbreviating of 'gang kill' in other words.

## Swashbuckling PR

An online fantasy role playing game might seem like an odd place to hold a press conference, even one with millions of members such as World of Warcraft, but that is exactly what happened on 1 December 2007. In the real world Ross Mayfield is the CEO of SocialText, a provider of online collaborative working tools for business. But it was a sword-wielding knight going by the name of Kalevipoeg who held court during the press conference within the virtual world. This 3D environment has proven to be a global phenomena not least because it manages to mix gaming with social networking, creating a virtual environment with attitude. That attitude was all too obvious at the press conference where the gathered reporters, represented by their own sword-wielding avatars of course, could only ask a question of Mayfield if they first challenged Kalevipoeg to a swashbuckling duel.

Not that the compulsive real-world Sarah is reflected in her World of Warcraft character 'if they start killing me, I will obviously fight back, and if I lose I will get reinforcements, but I wouldn't just kill people who are trying to get on'. Interestingly, when pushed on the ganking aspect of the game, Sarah admits to occasionally adopting a dark 'rogue' character and enjoying the experience 'if only because so many rogues ganked me when I was trying to level up, so I like to go into the battlegrounds and exact my revenge'.

But ultimately, it is the healing Rosmarus, the grown-up KiBo, the real Sarah that dominates her time in-world. 'I find it sad to think that anyone would want to hide behind an Internet persona forever, and kind of cruel to the people they befriend', Sarah admits. Which is probably why she isn't hiding at all . . .

Unlike Daisy, who has been hiding her entire life.

Indeed, Daisy isn't her real name, as anonymity was a prerequisite to allowing me to recount her story within these pages. Daisy has an online identity that she does not feel comfortable presenting to anyone other than her husband in the real world. Daisy is what is known as a spanko.

Daisy has an **online identity** that she does not **feel comfortable** presenting to anyone other than **her husband** in the **real world**

She has been struggling with the acceptance of her sexual fetish for years. Not just acceptance from work colleagues, family and friends as you might imagine either, but searching for self-acceptance even more than that of the world at large.

'My husband spanks me, and I enjoy it. I don't want to enjoy being spanked. I don't understand why I do. All I know is that I've thought about spanking for as long as I can remember. It is an aspect of myself that I am completely embarrassed about. While spanking is one of the more common fetishes, it is still something that I struggle with'.

Daisy, a graduate student, satisfies her passion for literature with her classmates and professors; she can be silly and have fun with her friends. In fact pretty much all of her needs – to be involved with and to talk about every aspect of her life – are satisfied in the real world.

Everything except spanking.

'It doesn't seem to fit in with any other aspect of my personality. I am a very inde-pendent woman; intelligent, educated, professional, capable, and can be assertive in areas where I feel confident of my abilities'. Daisy does not present herself as a submissive person to anyone other than her husband, and the people with whom she chats online. 'I doubt that any of my friends would realise that I enjoy being spanked by and being submissive to my husband. I certainly hope they don't realise this, because I fear they wouldn't understand'.

Perhaps it is because of a sexually repressive culture where sex is everywhere yet sexual fetishes of any kind are taboo? 'They are fodder for jokes, but no one seems to want to talk about them seriously, unless it is to say that these people must be damaged in some way'. Going through life considering herself a soli-tary 'freak', it wasn't until she stumbled across an online community of other spankos that Daisy started to discover herself. Chatting with these like-minded souls has become almost like group therapy: a group of people who understand how she thinks and feels, a group of people who will not and do not judge or laugh at her. 'While I still feel uncomfortable with this part of myself, I no longer feel alone'.

Not least because Daisy met her husband online, some eight years ago now.

'I explored various chat rooms available online, these tended to be focused on more taboo topics, mostly sexual. I found a spanking-themed chat room, although at this point I was still much too afraid to post anything'. Daisy didn't actually start communicating directly with the online spanking community until early 2007, in fact. 'There was a function that allowed you to see what people were in a chat room and check their profiles without entering the room yourself. This is how my husband found me. I had a quote from one of Shakespeare's plays in my profile, my future husband was highly educated and well-versed in Shakespeare. He instant messaged me and started a conversation about Shakespearean plays, it wasn't until later that we started talking about spanking'.

The couple chatted online during the course of the following year, but Daisy was cautious about giving too much personal information away, not least because many people are not honest. Whenever he would reveal any personal information, she would check it immediately. His claimed profession required him to be licensed, so Daisy checked his licensing information with the appropriate state authorities to make sure he was who he said he was, and when he gave her his company name she checked that out as well. It took 18 months for enough trust to be established for telephone numbers to be exchanged, and a further year of talking before a face-to-face meeting was arranged.

'It allowed me a feeling of safety that I never had with in-person courtships'.

Daisy, you see, is a survivor of long-term childhood sexual abuse.

> ▌▌ I frequently **feel** that my **real life identity** is a **façade**, and my **Internet** identity is **truer** to **who I really am** ▐▐

'My online courtship allowed me to feel safe because I knew that he could not violate me physically, and this feeling of safety allowed me to develop trust in him over the years I was getting to know him. I'm not sure that I would have been able to develop a healthy relationship with an in-person courtship, because I'm not sure that I would have been able to develop this trust if the possibility of physical intimacy was immediately and continuously present'.

Certainly social mores sometimes make it very difficult to communicate honestly for fear of being judged by the people you address. Walk into a room of strangers and there is no way of knowing which people will hold what opinions and who is likely to be offended or shocked by whichever line of questioning. Online it is just so much simpler to seek out people with similar life experiences, holding similar beliefs and with compatible life values. People of whom you can ask frank questions without feeling burdened by the weight of the worry of propriety.

'If I want to chat about spanking with people who have had similar experiences, I simply use a search engine to find spanking chat groups. I can just as easily seek out people who hold particular political views, academic interests, or just about anything else I choose to chat about'. And for Daisy this is absolutely vital, because she just does not possess the kind of thick skin required to be completely honest with people whose views and beliefs she doesn't know in advance. There is too much danger of inadvertently offending someone, or being judged for who she is. 'I frequently feel that my real life identity is a façade, and my Internet identity is truer to who I really am'.

I know only too well where Daisy is coming from. After all, my entire life up to the point I was blessed with being ravaged by a life-threatening brain virus had been something of a façade. A poorly child, weakened by recurring stomach upsets which in later life I was to discover were caused by food allergies, I concealed the scared little boy by becoming the class clown. It worked in as far as the bullies were happy for me to deliver the punchline instead of them lining up to punch me. Ever so briefly in my teenage years the most honest version of myself yet managed to appear when punk rock exploded onto the scene and let me throw off the shackles of parental expectation and school discipline. At once expressing a note of individualism while safely merging with the crowd. Shocking everyone, hurting nobody. I liked that a lot. So much that it is high on my list of preferred epitaphs.

Then I left school at the tender age of 16, against the advice of my teachers and the shattering the dreams of my parents. I didn't want to further my education; in typical 16-year-old fashion I felt I had learned enough. What I wanted was an income, so I left school and got a job. I also left behind my new-found freedom, the identity I had become at one with, in the historic buildings of Haberdashers Aske's Hatcham Grammar School for boys. The old Askean punk disappeared under a suit and tie, the real me drowning in a sea of responsibility. I adopted the guise of a grown-up on the outside, while feeling ever more the lost and lonely little boy within. I did what the world expected of me, I worked hard and I got married and I started a family and I took on a mortgage and I cried myself to sleep nearly every night.

The irony of the situation did not escape me. Here I was confined to a wheelchair, bound by the physical restrictions of my disability, yet with that same sense of freedom I last felt as a punk rocker. At least that was the case while I was online, when I escaped the prison cell of my miserable life. Yet I was discovering something in this brave new modem-powered world, a part of me that had long since been buried: a voice that demanded to be heard.

Although I had tried my hardest to fight the real-world depression that I would fall into from the very heights of elation just an hour or two before, I was losing the battle more than winning it. Every now and then depression hit me so hard there was simply no getting away from it. It was during one such visitation by the black dog that I discovered not only that I had this voice online, but people were listening as well. So it was I found myself musing about how bad my life was and that I had given it much thought and decided the time was right to end it all. I announced, in no uncertain terms, that I was going to kill myself. What happened next not only saved my life, but convinced me that the gap between the online and real world was not as great as everyone assumed.

# What **happened** next **not only saved my life** but **convinced** me that **the gap between the online and real** world was **not as great** as everyone **assumed**

Immediately there were people replying and offering help, offering to talk, offering to do whatever it took to prevent the same chap they had been arguing with and complaining about the day before from killing himself.

Within 10 minutes there was a knock on the front door and someone who happened to live just around the corner, unbeknownst to me at the time, had transported out of the virtual world and into my flat. Someone I had been verbally abusing online the previous week, for whom I had little virtual time and no real-world contact. Yet here he was, in my living room, removing the paracetamols bottle from my grip and literally saving my life.

An hour passed, as did my suicidal thoughts, and my flat found itself accommodating no less than half a dozen concerned online acquaintances. I remember at the time thinking it was really rather a special thing this world of online community where even the most annoying of participants can spark a genuine reaction with a heart-wrenchingly honest posting.

I kept the company of outsiders: geeks and nerds, bikers and punks. Virtual misfits one and all. The best friends I have ever had. The only real friends I ever needed.

The importance of the online world, the importance of CIX, in all this extends beyond being the place that saved my life, where the new me was conceived and educated. CIX was also directly responsible for my launch into the world of free-lance writing.

As well as attracting good Samaritans, CIX also attracted technology journalists. This was probably due in no little part to the good business decision by the owners of CIX to provide numerous journalists with free accounts, thus ensuring coverage in the computing press one way or another. Even if they were not writing about CIX, it was publicised thanks to them printing their email address as a contact point. Indeed, it was thanks to the proliferation of computer magazine editors on the system that I got my first freelance commission, before I even knew what one was.

Perhaps it was mere coincidence, but the realisation that the identity I was developing online was someone I rather liked preceded a remarkable change in my real-world circumstances.

The **realisation** that the **identity I was developing** online was **someone I rather liked** pre-empted **a remarkable change** in my real world **circumstances**

Along with a new-found sense of purpose, a love for life that had been missing for a year if truth be told, came a change in my health. Within 6 months I had regained the use of my left arm and progressed from lumbering electric wheelchair to lightweight sports model. One of the ways that my experience in the virtual world impacted very directly upon my behaviour in the real one, was better appreciating the power of my image.

I quickly came to the conclusion that, as well as being of little consequence when it came to understanding who someone really was, the person behind the mask as it were, one's appearance could actually act as a great twit filter. No more would I be bothered by the does he take sugar brigade, no more would I have to suffer at the tongues of the patronising classes.

So it was that I became the leather-clad, tattooed and pierced, Mohawk-wearing cyberpunk cripple. If that didn't scare off the shallow and bigoted morons then I didn't know what would. Although my birth certificate still said 'David Winder', it had been a long time since anyone had called me that, even my own mother used Dave instead. Post encephalitis, I didn't feel like a Dave any more, and as luck would have it, one of my new-found friends was a fan of the *Vic Reeves Big Night Out* comedy show which was being broadcast around the same time.

# The **cyberpunk in the wheelchair**, and his **online** manifestation that **roamed the virtual worlds**, had **found** a name: **David** Winder had become Wavey **Davey**

One of the surreal characters was a man who waved at people and things in an increasingly malevolent way as the shows progressed, and being revealed as Satan by the end. It was decided that some of my personas that were emerging online, especially in the wilder regions of the Usenet system, did a similar thing: greeting people in bizarre ways, engaging them in surreal conversations and often with an anarchic climax to the conversation.

The cyberpunk in the wheelchair, and his online manifestation that roamed the virtual worlds, had found a name: David Winder had become Wavey Davey.

## Usenet

Usenet was the bridge between the bulletin boards of old and the newly emerging Internet. A network of chat forums known as newsgroups, covering every topic imaginable, which formed the precursor to the web-based forums that exist today.

Yet dwindera was not dead; his character remained confined to CIX and continued to help and hinder members in equal measure. A strange thing started to happen: it appeared that even though most people knew it was the same person (and every message posted on CIX would be from the same account after all) they would refer to the helpful side of me as dwindera and the delinquent as Wavey. My emerging personality had been split, even if I had not purposefully split it myself.

After all, my virtual personalities were just a mirror to my real-world experiences: whatever was happening in my life was magnified, exaggerated and exploded into the online world. If I was feeling down in the dumps, online I was suicidal. If I was going through a manic phase, online I was simply out of control. If nothing else, I was always quite openly me even when pretending to be something or someone else. This probably requires some explanation and I will try my best to provide it.

Although the core identities of dwindera and Wavey Davey remained pretty constant, I found myself surrounded by numerous alternative personalities. Some of these lasted for many years, others were regarded as disposable and serving no purpose when whatever booze- or drug-fuelled mission they had been on was complete.

Upon discovering a chat forum inhabited purely by morris dancers, for example, I felt compelled to organise a mini-invasion of sorts where myself and a few friends all crashed into the discussion at a pre-determined time with the world's first online morris dance. In truth this consisted of nothing more than half a dozen drunken souls posting messages over a 20-minute period that said things such as 'jingle jingle jingle' and 'bangs stick, falls over'. No doubt it annoyed the heck out of the regular forum participants, but equally there can be no doubting we all found it hugely amusing at the time.

Online morris dancing was an incredibly immature thing to do, but that's exactly the point: in terms of identity, of personal growth, I was still that online child. I was pushing boundaries and trying to determine what I could and could not get away with. I was learning who I was. No, more than that, I was creating the new me.

## In terms of identity, of personal growth, I was still that online child

I was not alone, other online community pioneers were also exploring the edges of acceptable behaviour. Some 15 years after the event some members of CIX still talk about the day during a British Grand Prix when a user calling himself Nigel Mansell popped up in a technical support forum asking for help with his Internet connection that he kept losing as he went under the bridges. Some even responded to offer the most famous of British drivers at the time the help he so desperately requested, in the middle of a Grand Prix! Perhaps unsurprisingly, the man behind the Nigel Mansell prank and I became close friends, best friends in fact, and remain so until this day.

So here I was online, acting the idiot one minute and being a serious and helpful member of the community the next. The more serious side of my nature was reflected in my off-line life where I had become not only a member of the British Computer Society 'Disability Specialist Group', but also its membership secretary. This fact did not go unnoticed by one magazine editor on CIX, who emailed me out of the blue to ask if I would like to write a feature for Amiga Computing magazine which explained just how computers and cyberspace were changing the lives of disabled people.

I jumped at the chance, figuratively speaking, and produced my first ever piece of published work in 1991. Not bad for someone who, just a year before, had been unable to read or write, who had been written off by the medics and most of his friends, who seemingly had nothing to live for. Not bad at all, as it turns out. Reader feedback to the piece was so positive, and my brash writing style so refreshing at the time, that I was offered a monthly column as a direct result. My career as a writer had begun.

Around the same time I had taken a job as volunteer director of a public transport scheme for disabled people, South London Dial-A-Ride, and had thrown myself into the role of disability activist. At one meeting a producer from the newly formed Disability Programming Unit of the BBC was speaking. Naturally I gave her a hard time over the type of content being produced and was surprised when she approached me afterwards for a chat. During our conversation it was revealed that I was a fledgling journalist and lover of music, and she was looking for someone to script and present a 45-minute documentary about the disability music scene for the *Late Show* on BBC2.

One box in the search for a new identity could now be ticked, I was a writer and broadcaster no less. Not only was I growing up online, but the scared little boy in the real world had started to mature as well . . .

Not everyone was growing up online, in fact some were making a concerted effort to regress. A popular truism at the time was that on the Internet nobody knows you are a dog, and some people grasped the nettle of anonymity long enough to make a name for themselves if only virtually. Some people grasped the opportunity to have a laugh and live out their own fantasies simultaneously. Not many people managed to sustain the lie as long as Simon the virtual rock star though.

# On the **Internet** nobody **knows you are a dog**

It all started in 1991 when Simon was working as a cub reporter for the Western Daily Press in Bristol, sharing a house with his best friend from school. There was no nightlife in Tetbury at the time, so Simon and his friend created their own: they formed a band which didn't exist . . .

'The founding moment came when we asked a one-man band in an almost-empty pub to play us "The Green Green Grass of Home" by Tom Jones on his little Yamaha keyboard. It was about the most inappropriate song we could think of bar "Anarchy in the UK", which he'd already refused to do. To our horror, he agreed, on condition that we sing along'. Simon explained they couldn't because they were under contract and taking a night off from their UK tour. Quick as a flash, The Xenophobics came into being. Beyond deciding that he was a Hungarian drummer called Nesjo who spoke only a few words of heavily accented English, his mate morphed into Turnstier the surly guitarist looking after him, the plot never really thickened and The Xenophobics stagnated.

Until 1997.

'My wife was pregnant with our second son and my best friend had just met the woman who would become his wife 18 months later. My wife was staying abroad to avoid a rainy Manchester summer and I didn't want another summer holiday visiting her parents. I'm whingeing about the rain, and she suggests we go on a long-delayed lads' holiday. One week later we are on that holiday in some desolated village in Samos, probably the most family-friendly Greek island of all. The night-life made Tetbury look wild'.

'During a day trip to Turkey as part of a tour group of elderly Dutch folk, the tour guide cracks a joke about it being so hot he could feel a little bead of sweat rolling down between his cheeks. Nobody else on the bus even smiles, but in a moment of laughter-induced madness The Xenophobics were reformed, with the tour guide unknowingly co-opted as their virtual manager. Arriving back home the 'band' decide to change their name to "strawberry starfish" for typically laddish reasons involving a man on a nudist beach! Typing this into an online translation engine they come up with a German version, "Erdbeerseestern", and the band is officially renamed in an instant'.

'To nobody's surprise, erdbeerseestern.de was available, but we preferred the snazzier ebss.de, and I registered my first domain name. The band is taking shape and we are both excited by the idea of taking the joke as far as it will go'. So it was that Erdbeerseestern got a web page in August 1999, complete with a detailed back history stretching as far as 1982. 'Our creative output was phenomenal, we sometimes penned the lyrics to up to four or five songs a day'.

The creative output was also unique, as the lyric-writing style came courtesy of that same Babelfish language translation engine that had provided the unlikely-sounding band name. By taking an English lyric and translating it into German or

French and then back to English, an online hobby known as Babelfishing which became quite popular for a short time, the words would become pretty much unrecognisable. For example, Elvis Presley's 'There's No Room To Rhumba In A Sports Car' became '(Is There Not A Space To) Rhumba In A Sport Auto', one of the bands biggest hits.

'For a few glorious weeks in 2000 we were top of the charts: the first hit returned by MSN's search engine on the term "roof rafters", our special new track for the greatest hits album'.

When the band finally broke up in October 2003, the website hosted more than 30 pages, detailing a back catalogue of some 16 albums and as many singles, all replete with artwork and lyrics. 'Although we're not sure if anyone really believed us or not, we made it into lots of directories listing alternative rock bands, and there are still 80-plus results showing up today in Google'.

Simon certainly had a case of split online personality going on, but this was not a case of there being no connection, no control between real life and the virtual world. It was more a case of if the suit fits, wear it, and online the rock star

**Just some of the singles released by Erdbeerseestern, the band that never existed.**

leathers fitted perfectly. In terms of personality, I was trying on different clothes as well, as many different styles as possible to see which fitted me best of all. Of course, there was no best fit as it turned out, I was destined to become the sum of my parts: a composite persona built with a little from here and a little from there. One outfit that I could not change was my disability, it was a part of my wardrobe that was fixed whether I liked it or not, and it was helping to shape who I was becoming.

# 3 Enabling Technologies

**One thing I never did** was hide online, just the opposite. I certainly never hid behind my disability. In fact, while the small matter of my being disabled was no big secret, it was not something I shouted from the rooftops either. I would no more introduce myself as Davey the wheelchair user than I would Davey the pagan or Davey the English bloke. That was exactly the type of stereotyping I was escaping from in the real world. By the time people had decided I was an idiot it didn't really matter that I was a disabled idiot; the connection had already been made.

That was then, in an online age when words were all we had to paint the picture of a personality, when first impressions were not restricted to eye candy graphics and all the more valuable as a result. In the immersive 3D environment of the virtual worlds we inhabit today, it is all too easy to make a snap decision based upon looks, and just as easy to be totally wrong. If all you look at is the cover of a book, then how can you ever expect to enjoy the story as it unfolds across the pages within?

While you might imagine then, given the freedom of physical movement available in a 3D virtual world, every disabled user would choose an able-bodied avatar and fly everywhere, you would also be wrong. Of course, there are many who do just that, experiencing a freedom which goes far beyond anything the most physically able person could hope for on terra firma. After all, how many people do you know who can leap into the air and fly from place to place, soaring high above the crowds below? But that is far from the whole story. There are those for whom their disability is such an essential part of who they are, who have no compunction to 'escape' from themselves, who do not hide behind a mask of physical normality online.

Take Simon for example, a 33-year-old businessman from Coventry in the UK. A disability consultant and trainer by profession, Simon is also chief executive of Enable Enterprises and happens to have been born with cerebral palsy.

On 4 May 2006 Simon was introduced to Second Life by a work colleague, and became hooked. 'I very quickly met someone who gave me my first wheelchair'.

**Simon Stevens, virtual *Big Brother* contestant and Second Life nightclub owner.**

Which is ironic, because in real life Simon doesn't always use a wheelchair at all, but felt it important to be recognised as disabled in the virtual world in order to preserve his feeling of self-identity.

## Second Life

Second Life (www.secondlife.com) is a 3D virtual world where some 12 million members are represented on-screen by their avatar, and can interact with other avatars and the environment around them. Content such as clothing, transport and property is created and owned by the residents, who are free to sell these items to other avatars. Second Life has a booming in-world economy with more than a million real US dollars changing hands every single day. It is immersive in every sense, and everything that happens in the realm world is mirrored within. Second Lifers build businesses, fall in love, get married and even have sex with each other . . .

'Having cerebral palsy since birth means I have always been disabled and do not know how **not** to be. To save a lot of explanation, it was important to use a wheelchair'.

Pretty soon Simon was exploring the environment, and participating in the varied activities, including some sailing, for example. He also became more than a little interested in the social scene within Second Life and, in particular, the many clubs and bars that are scattered around the virtual world. 'I was not sleeping very well, but for the first time I had a social life where I had friends from all over the world. I was spending most nights in Second Life and this was greatly helping with the depression I was going through'.

Back in the early days of its existence, the Second Life community was very much smaller and certainly a lot less diverse than it is today. 'In those days I seemed to be the only wheelchair user, and people asked a lot of questions about my use of the wheelchair. Question like was I disabled in real life and why did I use a virtual wheelchair when I did not need to? Some people complained I was not "playing the game" properly'. Things have changed since then, and there are now a lot more wheelchair-using Second Life residents, and with this more diverse demographic comes a greater acceptance of disability within the community.

## Some **people** complained I was **not "playing the game" properly**

Simon, being rather business-savvy, soon realised the real world commercial potential of the virtual environment. He had an idea that there might be sufficient demand for a disability issues training centre which could operate to the benefit of companies in real life and Second Life alike. He also thought it might be fun to set up a virtual nightclub called Wheelies.

'Everyone was setting up nightclubs at that time, and what would a disabled person call his nightclub but Wheelies? It started just as a daft idea, but after the official launch on 1st September 2006 I quickly realised that Wheelies was a lot bigger than I ever expected. It had a real community purpose. Everyone who comes to Wheelies, disabled or not, always seem to have a disability story which the club helps them explore within a safe environment'.

Having been selected to participate in the Second Life version of *Big Brother*, Simon's profile was about to get raised even higher.

## Big Brother

Produced by the same company as is behind the hit television series *Endemol*, *Big Brother* came to Second Life on 1 December 2006. Fifteen resident avatars had to spend at least 8 hours a day online, in a big glass house, under the watchful eye of Second Life users across the world who would vote for evictions at the end of each week. In a grand finale on 4 January 2007, the winner received a virtual tropical island of her own.

What better publicity for a nightclub than appearing on *Big Brother*? No matter if the screen upon which it airs is of the television or computer variety. Unfortunately for Simon, real-world prejudices and jealousies reared their ugly heads and, just as everything seemed to be going so well, brought his clubbing empire literally crashing down around his knees. The day after leaving the *Big Brother* house, that illusion of prosperity was shattered as Wheelies was subjected to an in-world griefing attack which saw the club destroyed. It took a few months for Simon to recover from this setback, selling some of his Second Life land and generally just chilling out while he considered what to do next.

## Griefing

According to Wikipedia, griefing is a slang term used to describe a player in a multiplayer game who plays 'simply to cause grief to other players through harassment'. This can be anything from relatively harmless but annoying avatar stalking, through to the detonation of in-world bombs. Second Life *Big Brother* was 'griefed' on the opening night when residents had to walk a red carpet to enter the house. Unfortunately the avatars were caged, and then set on fire. Being a virtual environment, no permanent damage was done. At the other end of the griefing scale, virtual terrorist organisations such as the Second Life Liberation Army have emerged to carry out bombings of corporate concerns in-world, which they see as an infringement of the democratic rights of individual avatars. The SLLA set off virtual bombs outside a Reebok store to launch its campaign.

'It was amazing how during this period the spirit of Wheelies lived on and the club was still being blogged about despite not actually existing'. Simon's mind was made up: 'I reopened Wheelies'. Within six months it was bigger than ever, and has become very much a cornerstone as far as both Second Life clubbing and community is concerned, having been featured in *Newsweek* magazine, on CNN and the BBC. 'Wheelies has also become a focal point for disabled users and wheelchair users, as well as non-disabled people, who want to have a good time within a safe environment. I plan to ensure that Wheelies remains an important element to disability issues within Second Life'.

Like Simon, Buddy was born with cerebral palsy. Unlike Simon, however, 24-year-old Buddy does require the use of an electric powered wheelchair all the time. The model of a proud gay man, Buddy is used to not hiding who he is. Yet in the virtual world of There.com he does not see any reason why his avatar should be disabled. Buddy is Buddy: the wheelchair does not define him; it is merely a tool. A tool he does not need when immersed in what he likes to refer to as the 'online world community'.

## There.com

There.com is another of the 3D virtual worlds inhabited by avatars, but one where the creation of content is tightly controlled by the company that operates it. So while businesses exist that design and sell clothes, BBQs and hoverbikes, you won't find the kind of red light trading districts that flourish within Second Life for example. You will find that Thereians immerse themselves in their world as deeply as any other virtual voyagers.

**Wheelies has become a cornerstone of the Second Life clubbing scene.**

Buddy had got himself caught up in the world of online gaming by agreeing to sign on as a beta tester when the popular life simulation, The Sims, went online. It was fun, but it did not fulfil the desire that he had to find and participate fully within a social-based online cultural group where he could do more than just hang out, where he was not just part of a game. Buddy longed for a place where he could find a very real community, a place where he could find a sense of belonging and acceptance. Within a year he discovered There.com and, although he didn't realise it immediately, his life was about to change forever.

**There.com holds your hand as you enter the virtual world.**

'I joined the public beta for There.com in February 2003, and found it both extraordinary and intriguing to discover that everyone was not just an avatar. There was an actual personality behind each and every one and the community affords the opportunity to meet so many different types of personalities from all walks of life.' As far as Buddy was concerned, there was no need to reinvent himself online. 'I am very much the same person in that virtual world as I am in real life. I am always open about my disability.'

This environment quickly overrides any real-world stereotyping which has a habit of depicting a disabled person as either stupid or just plain unapproachable.

**There.com residents ensure there is always someone to talk to.**

Believe me, my years spent in a wheelchair taught me that quickly enough. The first time any disabled person experiences life within the virtual community of an online world, they are nearly always taken aback by the way that it removes the barriers of patronising convention so often encountered in real life when trying to form new friendships. It is not that people mean to be patronising, and usually do not even realise that they are, but there is what can only be described as a cultural if not generic imprinting to treat disability as a weakness, and weakness as requiring protection, and giving protection as taking control. The jump from meeting a disabled person to taking control over the relationship is usually a very small one.

**Buddy finds a freedom online where his wheelchair does not define him.**

IMAGE COURTESY OF THERE.COM

Online things are very different, and it is nearly all to do with perception. Take away the visual distraction of physical appearance and replace it with a direct line of sight into the thoughts, emotions and underlying personality of the human being instead and things become a whole lot better. 'Most members of the community get to know the person behind the avatar before they become aware of any disability, they are learning from the disabled population online that we are all equal'.

Buddy is passionate about the problems of perception and prejudice: 'Being disabled is cool: we get it, realise just being who we are is beautiful. We are beautiful in an imperfect world caught up in self-image and self-preservation'. And this is where virtual worlds such as There.com enter the picture, gracefully guiding newcomers to gradually understand the beauty of community, in all its guises, and embrace the unknown instead of fearing it. 'There.com cushions, in a dignified smooth and easy fashion, the initial introduction into my world of the disabled'.

**▲▲** There.com **cushions**, in a **dignified smooth** and **easy fashion**, the initial **introduction** into my **world of the disabled**

Once you get to know Buddy, this passion is easy to understand. For it is in the virtual world that he has made some of his most precious friendships. Friendships which have beautifully transitioned across into the real world.

Friends like Rob and Rory.

'Four years ago, I became particularly fond of a member I had just met and a priceless friendship began to evolve right before our eyes. We shared many common interests, but the biggest element that really made me feel comfortable was the compassion and acceptance that I had felt from him. We began to communicate in real life as well and three years later I met this member and his partner in real life. Everything I had already felt about both of them regarding their integrity had been confirmed'. Buddy's mother, a single parent, also took note to the attentiveness Rob and Rory had shown to her son, and immediately felt a connection. Rob and Rory visited Buddy at his New Jersey home the following year, and were faced with one of the most difficult conversations anyone could possibly imagine.

Buddy's mother asked if they would be prepared to take responsibility for their friend should anything happen to her. Discussions and planning for the care of someone who is severely physically challenged when faced with the inevitable truth of separation was never going to be easy. But Rob and Rory were quick to ensure that Buddy and his mother did not feel alone anymore, and so, at the start of 2007 mother and son upped sticks and moved across the US from New Jersey to Costa Mesa, California to be closer to their friends from Long Beach. 'We love each other like brothers, and the move to California was definitely the right thing to do. It provided me with the security that I needed to sleep at night to know that I would be in good hands and that our friendship is reinforced by a bond that started virtually, and transformed all of our lives'.

Buddy is in absolutely no doubt that he has no one else to thank for making this happen other than the virtual community of There.com. 'I have friends with similar interests, I have guardian angels, and most importantly I am treated with the same dignity and respect that I am treated in real life. The friendships I have made in There.com, both online and in real life are all truly invaluable. Had it not been for other gay friends that I have made within There.com and then met in real life, both able-bodied and disabled, I definitely would not have the amount of confidence and the "stride in my step" that I do today. Not only has There.com changed my life and my future, it has also given me the confidence to fully embrace who I am in every possible capacity and not be afraid of persecution'.

**❝ Not only** has **There.com** changed my **life** and my **future**, it has **also given me** the **confidence** to fully embrace who I am **❞**

There.com has also played a big part in the life of Greg, a former mechanic employed to keep the heating, air conditioning and plumbing up and running at a local college in Ontario, Canada. Greg led a very tactile life. He had a passion for fixing cars and off road motorcycling. He had plans for the future.

And he had ocular histoplasmosis.

Doctors tried to prevent the disease from spreading, but despite myriad laser treatments his sight continued to deteriorate and Greg was declared legally blind in 1990.

'After becoming legally blind, I was unable to work at the job I had been doing, was unable to drive my car, could not read newspaper sized print, and unable to do many day to day things that people do and take for granted such as comparing prices on items in the grocery store. I was suddenly living a totally different life. It was a devastating time for me'.

Greg's friends were, of course, both sympathetic and supportive. However, he could no longer participate in the same activities, could not drive his car in order to visit them. 'The way I had to live my life because of my visual impairment created a social impairment. I grieved over the loss of most of my vision for several months and then decided I needed to rearrange my life'.

Greg went back to school, taking computer courses, and eventually earning several certifications in computer programming. With help from local agencies he managed to acquire a computer replete with the adaptive hardware and software to enable him to use it properly. 'I started building web pages, I played online games, discovered instant messaging and email, and gained some of my freedom back'.

Discovering There.com in 2005, Greg did not take long to become totally addicted to the freedoms he found within. 'While in There.com, I can drive, fly, and ride

**Greg lives two lives that seldom intersect, and it's in the virtual one he has found fame and fortune.**

vehicles. This is very freeing to me since I can't enjoy the same in real life'. It should come as no surprise, then, that after spending time in There and then going back to the real world, Greg is anxious to return. 'Back in my real life I settle into the routine of coping with the day to day rituals. I lead two lives that seldom intersect'.

He understands that his virtual life is taking place in a 'game' and is more than capable of separating reality from virtuality. That does not prevent him from wanting to be able to bring the freedoms of his virtual existence into his real life. 'It's hard to explain the value I get from my online experience to someone who does not experience it'.

Another hard-to-explain concept is that of the virtual economy, but Greg picked up on this from very early on and decided he wanted to try a little bit of virtual wealth creation for himself. He achieved this by using his new-found computing and design skills to create content which can be sold to other There.com residents: a beer cooler perhaps, or how about a flashy BBQ? In fact, Greg's items command good prices at in-world auctions and have become amazingly popular. As well as bringing a certain amount of virtual wealth, this success has also brought notoriety. It has made his There.com alter ego, Kortt, famous.

'The notoriety I've gained in a virtual world is astonishing and sometimes overwhelming. I sometimes have people meet me and say "Wow, I really like your stuff" and "I can't believe I'm getting to meet you" whereas in real life I have no notoriety, in fact I'm one of the most anonymous people around'. This has endowed Greg with a renewed sense of being someone again. Someone who makes a difference, someone who matters, someone who lives rather than just exists.

There's plenty of fun to be had in There.com, all the fun of the fair if you want it.

IMAGE COURTESY OF THERE.COM

The competitive avatar can even race against other residents in a virtual buggy.

IMAGE COURTESY OF THERE.COM

> ❝ The **notoriety I've gained** in a virtual world is **astonishing** and sometimes **overwhelming** ❞

'In real life I feel exactly the way I am: disabled and sometimes lost. I must rely on others to help me do things. While in There.com I'm completely self sufficient. I don't think it can be explained, I think it must be experienced to fully understand the impact a virtual life can have on your real life. In that real life I may meet someone, exchange the usual pleasantries, and feel compelled to state that I have a visual impairment'.

> ❝ It must be **experienced** to **fully** understand **the impact a virtual life** can have on your **real life** ❞

Greg has no central vision and can only use his peripheral vision, so in order to see someone's face he has either to be very close or look off to one side. 'I have developed a sort of humorous litany to explain this to them, starting with "Don't be alarmed if I seem to be looking behind you. . . . " In the virtual world I do not feel the need to explain my disability straight away. Where a conversation is taking place with voice chat I show no outward appearance that anything is different, if the conversation is text driven I will have to explain my situation. Most often my virtual friends will jump in and explain that "Kortt can't see your text, he has a visual impairment"'.

Some people play online games, visit virtual worlds, in order to escape from reality and become someone they are not in real life. Greg does not have a different personality online, although he readily admits it is a much happier one. 'I try to keep the values I have in real life such and honesty and kindness, in my virtual life. I think I've been successful so far'.

# 4 With This Click, I Thee Wed

**Greg found happiness online with** his honest and kind avatar, Kortt, through creating objects, contributing to the community that has made him feel worthy once more. He leaves behind an anonymous existence to become someone online. Some people are looking for a whole lot more. Some people are looking for love.

The media laps up stories of Internet dating and cybersex relationships, eager to parade the characters in their tales like some kind of exhibits in a freak show. Yet these people are only using the Internet as a method of communication, a way to reach out and find a soulmate. We live in a global village now; the gene pool quest is not restricted by the limitations of travel. Couples are free to fall in love no matter where they live or work, and that is a beautiful thing, a thing worthy of celebrating surely?

But can the same be said when two people who have never actually met, who have not felt the touch of a hand or heard the softness of a whispered 'I love you' and who know nothing of each others lives beyond the cartoon façade exhibited within a virtual world, declare undying love for each other? What has happened to us as a society, as a culture, when our real lives have become so empty of emotional satisfaction, so bereft of romance that we seek out happiness in the arms of an avatar?

The answer to this question largely depends upon whether you consider your time within a virtual world as simply playing a game or somehow immersing yourself in a parallel universe, a real life lived through the computer screen. My conversations with numerous in-world-only couples suggests that they fall into two distinct camps: game players and deceivers.

## In-world

In order to prevent confusion between reality and virtuality, people talk about events that happen 'in-world' for avatar-related incidents and 'In Real Life' or simply IRL for the real-world stuff.

The vast majority would appear to treat their in-world marriage as just another bit of role playing, one more quest completed in the game, one more step towards making it feel even more real. Who can blame them? If you play an immersive 3D game on the kind of scale that is presented by the likes of Second Life, then it stands to reason that your immersion is everything.

However, there are plenty of in-world-only couples who, when you talk to them off the record and individually of each other, admit that they have 'fallen in love' and want to be able to bridge the gap between the fantasy and reality. The unrequited lover continues to play the game, continues the deceit, in an ever more desperate attempt to get closer to the object of their affection. Object being the operative word, because without a degree of communication away from the context of the game, outside of that virtual environment, how can anyone truly get to know the real person behind the screen?

But is this really that different from the way so many of us live our lives out here In Real Life? We work in little boxes, live in little boxes, and only know our colleagues and neighbours on a nod-of-the-head basis. Is there not an argument to suggest that by immersing ourselves within a virtual world at least we are meeting new people, making new friends, socialising and communicating with someone, with anyone?

Well yes, perhaps that might be the case if we were talking purely about lonely people denied the opportunity to discover romance because of their circumstances. There is even a suggestion that the people who enter into any long-distance relationship are, at some subconscious level, scared of commitment,

**Romance can start with a simple buggy ride in There.com.**

scared of the risk of rejection that closeness opens up. However, there is no end of well-documented cases of people involved in just this kind of virtual domesticity who have real wives in their real lives.

Take Ric, a man with two wives, one of whom he has never met in real life nor even spoken to on the telephone. Yet Ric and Janet have a mortgage, two dogs, and spend hours taking long motorcycle rides – in Second Life. According to a story in the online *Wall Street Journal* ('Is This Man Cheating on His Wife?') when Ric needed cheering up following some real life surgery Janet bought him a private island for 120,000 Linden Dollars. Unsurprisingly his real wife of less than a year, Sue, is none too pleased with there being another woman in his life, virtual or otherwise. She is quoted as saying that 'You try to talk to someone or bring them a drink, and they'll be having sex with a cartoon, which you have to imagine could perhaps have a detrimental effect upon a relationship.

**Or maybe a more traditional dance is more your virtual dating style?**

IMAGE COURTESY OF THERE.COM

 You try to **talk to someone** or bring them a **drink**, and they'll be having **sex with a cartoon**

Of course, there are real love stories that happen in the virtual world. There are folk who fall for an avatar and develop a meaningful relationship that crosses over into real life. There are people like Rhonda and Paul, avatars like Heart Wishbringer and Joe Stravinsky.

Rhonda is a divorced single mother raising her three daughters in California. Having spent the majority of her time on this planet wondering what she wants to

**Heart Wishbringer and Joe Stravinsky'.**

be when she grows up, Rhonda considers herself a fairly average kind of a person. But she has anything but an average story to tell. At the age of 38 most women have careers and a home to call their own, Rhonda does not. She has her beautiful daughters for sure, but has been unsuccessful in finding a career because both of her previous relationships led her to work around their schedules. 'I worked odd jobs, odd hours and took care of the home' is a footnote of life that many women will find has resonance for them.

When her marriage broke up, Rhonda found herself moving to Pennsylvania with her significant other Dan, some 3000 miles from her closest family and equally distant from most of her friends. 'I never minded moving, I loved to travel and see places, so I went happily and was amazed at the beauty there', Rhonda explains 'I was very much in love, but I still felt very lonely. I always felt like I loved him more than he loved me. I used to spend many nights sleeping on the couch, crying myself to sleep because he would reject me when I wanted affection. I would ask myself if I could live with someone the rest of my life who made me feel so empty inside. I always told myself that I loved him, and that I could manage, always hoping he'd love me back the same'.

Rhonda had a best friend in Mimi, but she was in another state so they hung out together online for company, sometimes by way of a webcam and sometimes in Second Life. 'Since I didn't know anyone where I lived, and since I'm an introvert, I found it much easier to socialize online with the people who were from my real life but who lived miles away. I could log onto Second Life and hang out with my best friend. I also had other online friends who meant a lot to me, and I could hang out with them too'. In Second Life this lonely lady found a social life that she simply could not find in Pennsylvania. Being sans broadband and using a very old computer, the experience was tainted by her lack-of-cutting-edge kit. So it was that a new computer was purchased, a new broadband connection sub-scribed to, and a new life began.

'I didn't yet realise what kind of an impact it would have on my life. I didn't realise the potential it had. I spent the first week on Second Life trying to figure out what there was to do and see. I found out that I could go shopping for things for my avatar to wear'. She tried to make her cartoon self look like the real Rhonda at first, 'blonde and tan with big boobs'. But Rhonda soon discovered that she didn't like looking at a mirror of herself. This was a fantasy land, so why not shop for a new look? 'What I ended up with was a very short, athletic build character, with small breasts and a big butt, everything that was nothing like me in real life. I gave her black hair and pale white skin the colour of a sheet of printer paper. Her body had tribal tattoos all over it and her lips were full and deep red. I loved looking at her. The contrast was beautiful. She only ever wore red, white or black. I sculpted a beautiful body for her and purchased my hair, skin, clothing, shoes and jewellery'.

> **"** What I **ended up with** was a very **short**, **athletic build character**, with small **breasts** and a **big butt**, **everything** that was **nothing like me** in real life **"**

Shopping for life soon unmasked a problem, in order to continue purchasing more things to shape her online identity, Rhonda needed to get an online income. Luckily for her, she had made a friend called Striker who was teaching her how to navigate the virtual world.

**▌▌** It felt as **real** as any **virtual place** could, **it sucked me in** and I was **addicted** ▌▌

Striker was soon also teaching Rhonda how to make money in Second Life by entering and winning dance competitions. 'For the first month on Second Life all we did was go to dance competitions . . . go to the ones that interested us the most and paid the highest amount of Lindens. Together, he and I won almost every event. I was sitting in my recliner at home watching my avatar dance with Striker and listening to some really awesome music. I might have been sitting in a 100 year old home in Pennsylvania in the middle of winter with 3 feet of snow outside, bundled up with a blanket and waiting for Dan to come home, but online I was in a dance club, with friends, listening to music and laughing. The colours on my screen, the flashing lights, the DJ's playing songs dedicated to us and all our virtual friends envying us, how could I not smile? It felt as real as any virtual place could, it sucked me in and I was addicted'.

### Linden Dollars

Linden Dollars (L$) are the currency of Second Life, and the basis of a virtual economy in which the cash changes hands between residents as they buy and sell goods and services one avatar to another. Lindens, as they are known, can be bought and sold for US Dollars on the Lindex currency exchange. With more than $1 million being traded in Second Life every day, and a Gross Domestic Product (GDP) in excess of £100 million, this virtual economy is in better shape than many real-world ones . . .

The real world, however, was not such a happy place. Rhonda would get up from her recliner and walk about the house, wiping down counters and sweeping the floor, looking out the windows and wondering when Dan would get home. He worked the late shift as a correctional officer at the local jail. 'I always sort of sat next to him with my hands together on my knees and listened to him tell about his night. I'd wait patiently for him to get into bed beside me, and when he did he'd climb in and roll over. I usually sat there for a moment wondering why he didn't want to put his arms around me. I would take my pillow downstairs to the couch and put a blanket around me instead, I would go to the couch where I could cry and wonder what was wrong with me'.

Rhonda never shared her sadness with her online friends; Second Life was a happy place, a place that lived up to the promise of its name. At least for most of the time. Her real life best friend, Mimi, was spending an increasing amount of time in Second Life with the men that she met there and less time with Rhonda. When they spoke on the telephone she wanted to talk about the men that were falling in love with her there, how much fun she was having. 'We ended up having a fight over it and I needed to distance myself from her, because I didn't like that she had this wonderful husband at home, and she still wasn't satisfied and needed men online to make her happy too'.

The truth was that Rhonda would have loved to have had a man that showed her the kind of affection that Mimi got from her husband. 'If I had that, I'd be happy forever'.

And then Rhonda met Paul. Or more accurately, Heart met Joe.

It was 11 January 2005 at yet another dance event. Striker was with his virtual girlfriend and Heart was looking around the dance floor when her eyes fell upon Joe. 'There in front of me, past all the other people at the back of the room was this avatar. I had never seen anything like it before. He was amazing to look at, the tallest avatar I ever had seen. The first thing I noticed was his boots . . . better than any boots I had ever seen on a man yet. I glanced up and he wore tight shiny black leather pants and his skin was almost as white as mine . . . stark white, his chest was almost bare except for the wet t-shirt he had on that was clinging to his skin, the shirt as white as he was . . . yet defined. His face was stark white again and his eyes had dark black circles around them, his eyes were red snake eyes on black, his lips were black and he had vampire fangs and his hair was a very long beautiful white Mohawk. I just sat there in awe. This man was artistic, his avatar was original and unique. Red, White, Black . . . My lips turned upwards into an evil smile as I clicked on him to read his profile'.

It simply said 'I like cheese'.

Rhonda laughed and sent Joe a private message telling him how beautiful his avatar was. From here on in, the lives of Heart and Rhonda would be changed forever. That very night, during the dancing, Heart and Joe spent a lot of time talking to each other.

After the dance Striker and his girlfriend, along with Heart and Joe, headed for the virtual waterfalls and a moonlit chat. 'Every now and again he would send a snapshot he took of me. I just smiled and told him that taking photographs was one of my most favourite things to do in Second Life. I enjoyed the beauty of it. It was one of his favourite things to do too'. The couple would soon realise that they had a lot in common not only in Second Life, but in life as well.

Rhonda was honest and open with Paul, the man behind the Joe avatar, from the get go. This was not the stereotypical virtual fling, the kind of seedy cybersexual encounter so beloved by the tabloid media. This was different, this was a blossoming online friendship.

## Second Life Photography

One of the cool things about this virtual world is that you can share your experiences of it with other residents, as well as non-resident family and friends, just by using the built-in snapshot feature. Press a button on the interface toolbar and it's like taking a digital photo which can then be saved to your hard drive or sent as an email postcard to anyone you like.

'I told Paul from the very beginning that I had a boyfriend, and that I was very in love. I never said a bad thing about Dan'. Although Heart and Joe quickly became friends and confidants, they didn't actually spend that much time together in Second Life.

Heart was always rushing off to some dance competition with Striker to earn those Linden dollars, or trying to find the time to chat with all her other virtual friends. 'But when I did get a message from Joe I was always finding myself in awe with his sincerity and kindness. I remember many times thinking about him when I wasn't with him, and wondering how he was. I realised right away that I was genuinely interested in knowing him'. It appeared that Joe did not feel the same, because every time the two did chat, Heart had to re-approve her calling card. 'I didn't know what to make of it, and I didn't understand why he kept deleting my card'.

## Calling Cards

Unlike most Instant Message service buddy lists where someone is either added as a friend or not, the Second Life calling card system offers an in-between. Calling cards enable you to keep track of, and in touch with, people you might consider acquaintances and could become friends in the fullness of time. People you want to get to know better . . .

It turns out that Paul simply didn't think that Rhonda was serious about their friendship, what with always being so busy with other people and all. He was not the type of person to keep many cards, so he removed the ones that didn't keep in touch, usually just before she got in touch again.

Rhonda instinctively felt there was more to it than just this, that he liked her and rather than risk being hurt, would remove the card so as not to think of her. 'I didn't want to hurt him so told him that I wanted nothing more than a friendship. I believed this myself. I was in love, I was happy. Wasn't I?'

One day Heart promised she would spend some more time with Joe and the two went together to a very secluded place, a box in the sky that Paul had built, and the two chatted for many hours. 'I sat there in my recliner and had a very nice talk with a man on the other side of the world. I learned more about him . . . I learned that he was from Wales, I learned that he had two sons, and had never been married, I learned that for the most part he raised his sons on his own, I learned he used to be a painter and decorator but that now he stayed home full time to care for his autistic son, I learned he had a sometimes off and on relationship with a girl in his town, but it wasn't anything serious'.

Then it was time for Paul to learn about Rhonda, the real person behind the avatar. She explained all the things that made her happy, nothing negative, until Paul asked the big question 'Are you really happy?' This opened the door to the truth, about how lonely Rhonda really felt, how the emptiness never really went away. 'We had so much in common, so many times during our talks we were saying "me too" but amazingly I still never realised how much I needed this, I didn't realise the impact it would have on me. Letting someone in and letting them know not just the good, but the bad too. It felt like a weight came off of my shoulders'.

Rhonda decided to go to therapy. It didn't work out. Talking to a doctor was not the same as talking to Joe. 'I only liked letting Joe in. I liked his advice and I liked how much he cared about me'.

Then a surreal thing happened, the kind of thing that can only happen in surreal environment such as Second Life. An avatar friend who had broken up with his virtual wife wanted to make her jealous, wanted to win her back. He asked Heart if she would pretend to be his new girlfriend, and to make it convincing break her ties with all her other male friends in-world.

'I told Paul that I was going to be Kevin's girlfriend. I didn't mean as an "in love" girlfriend, I didn't take that stuff seriously. I didn't understand how anyone really could, no one really knew each other. It was like a soap opera you could live out online, and I was going to play a role. It was all drama I didn't really want to be involved in but Kevin knew that no other girl in his circle of friends could be more convincing, seeing as how I was well known to be the good girl in the group, the one that never fooled around with other girl's men in-world. I was not a cyber slut and I didn't want that kind of reputation, so I made sure that I didn't act like one'.

**❝ It was** like a **soap opera** you could **live out** online, **and** I was **going** to **play a role ❞**

Heart played the role, but Rhonda was bored out of her mind. She spent a lot of time wondering what Joe was doing, telling herself that what she was doing was stupid.

Heart missed Joe, a lot.

'I didn't know why I missed him so much but I instinctively knew that I needed him, I needed him right then. I was not enjoying my time at the Second Life pool party and I was bored at home in real life too. I'll never forget looking at the clock and thinking I could be doing better things with my time than pretending to be some guy's girlfriend in a game'.

When the party ended and everyone went off their separate virtual ways, Heart stood next to the pool, paced up and down beside the pool, while Rhonda sat in her recliner wondering what she was doing there, daydreaming at the screen and pondering the feelings inside.

'I felt it, it was there . . . I missed Joe. I kept thinking, could it be, was I falling for a guy in a game? I couldn't be addicted to him, we hadn't even done much together but talk, and I wasn't looking for anything more'. But Rhonda wanted to send him a private message, but what would she say? What could she say? How could she say anything? After all, she had just told him she was going to be Kevin's girlfriend, she didn't explain it, didn't make excuses, just told Joe that they needed to cut ties. 'I didn't really go into it, it was all just a game that I went along with. But, I felt sad, and I missed Joe . . . and I could feel a terrible sense of regret inside me. Why was I feeling like this? I thought it would be so easy to just cut ties with a guy online . . . but it wasn't it wasn't at all'.

> ❝ I missed **Joe.** I kept **thinking, could it be**, was I **falling for a guy** in a game? ❞

Rhonda sat in her chair, fiddling with her mouse and walking her avatar around whilst all the time contemplating just what it was she could be feeling. Contemplating just what she could say to him that would express those feelings. But before she could send a private message of any sort, Paul sent her one: 'I need you to love me, and I want you to need me'.

'My heart began to beat fast, I could feel something ripping apart inside of me and I felt as if that emptiness I always had just exploded and disappeared. There in front of me in an instant message from a man who was deeply on my mind were the words I had longed to hear for my entire life'.

At that moment, with those words from Paul in her message box, Rhonda began to cry.

She replied to him, and he came down from the sky where he had been floating up above, watching Heart the whole time. In real life Paul was sitting at his computer in Wales, crying as his heart was being broken before his very eyes. 'He had fallen in love with me, and I realised then that the love I wanted and needed was here right before me in the arms of an avatar'.

## " I realised then that the love I wanted and needed was here right before me in the arms of an avatar "

At that moment, as Joe floated down from above, and Heart fell to her knees, Rhonda instinctively knew that she had found something with this man that she had never experienced with anyone else.

The very next day Heart decided that she would spend all her time within Second Life in the company of the 7' 9" vampire who loved her. She would wrap her avatar around him like a koala bear holding onto a Eucalyptus tree. 'He took me to his castle and I stayed beside him, I reassured him that I wouldn't go. . . . We did nothing more intimate than cuddling and we spent a lot of time talking about why we were feeling the way we were. Why was it that we were making each other feel so whole, and so happy? Why was it that the love we felt here in Second Life felt so real and was so all-encompassing?'

As the days passed, Rhonda knew it was because she really was in love with this man whose voice she had never heard, whose real face she had never seen.

The 2 weeks they had known each other online seemed like forever. 'We decided we should talk, and show pictures of each other. I'll never forget the first time I heard his voice. He was so soft spoken and kind in his manner. I felt overwhelmed by his voice, and I spent a lot of time smiling. How could I find love online when I was in love in real life?'

The answer can be summed up as you don't know what you've been missing until it arrives. How could Rhonda have known that she was going to find what she had always wanted and needed within the bits and bytes of a virtual world? 'I spent so much time convincing myself that my relationship was wonderful with Dan because I felt so in love with him that I blinded myself and hid away the sadness of what it really was. I was in love with a man in real life that couldn't fulfil my needs. It wasn't until I met Paul in Second Life that I realised that'.

Heart and Joe had met at a Second Life dance on 11 January, just 20 days later on 31 January 2005 they eloped to the top of the waterfalls and got married within the virtual world.

**Heart decided she would spend her time in the company of the 7'9" vampire who loved her.**

# 20 days **later** on 31 January 2005 they **eloped** to the **top of the waterfalls** and got **married within the virtual world**

It was a private ceremony, just Heart and Joe and the priest. Not for them the media-driven event that many an online marriage has been, this was no sham, and by keeping the virtual marriage ceremony private they also kept it real. Or as real as a virtual relationship can ever hope to be. 'I'd stay in Second Life all day long, I even stayed there when Dan got home. I stayed as long as Paul was there. I stayed and he shared his life with me'.

**The quickest way to an avatar's heart is through her shoes.**

Paul also shared his talents at making shoes, virtual shoes that is. When Rhonda asked him to make her a pair as she didn't like any she could buy in the game, he obliged by crafting a pair of black and metal gothic ones.

'Everywhere I went in-world I received compliments on the shoes. I always had to tell them that they were made for me by my husband in Second Life, Joe Stravinsky . . . and that I loved them too'.

There were already some businesses that had set up shop selling virtual goods in Second Life, and it occurred to Rhonda that it might be possible to earn some real-life money selling these shoes that everyone so loved. The great thing about computer worlds is that it costs nothing to duplicate an item you have created and sell it over and over again. 'I thought what if we could sell these shoes and earn money to be together? I told Paul my thoughts and he and I both wondered if it would be possible to earn enough real life money to help us out of our situations in real life, help us to get together. It was a dream that we were not sure would come true'.

And so it was that Hearts Desire was born, a virtual store selling punky gothic style shoes and boots for the discerning avatar. 'The customers fell in love with our love story and they knew we wanted to be together more than anything, so they would come back again and again and bring their friends. We spent more time together and talking to each other than most real-life couples do. I don't think anyone I've ever known has had a relationship as open and as committed as we have had in this virtual world'.

> **We** spent **more time together** and **talking to each other** than most **real life couples** do

Back in the real world Dan continued to come home from work and be indifferent as Heart continued to be in Joe's virtual avatar arms. Rhonda even told him she had got married to Joe in the virtual world. 'He gave me a funny look and that was it. He thought it was stupid. He didn't find Second Life interesting at all'. Truth be told he didn't find Rhonda interesting at all anymore either, and moved off to North Carolina a month later. 'I stayed behind in Pennsylvania and continued my romance with Paul. But I needed Dan, if I didn't have Dan who would I have? I had no friends, no family. I was stuck.'

Rhonda ended up moving to North Carolina after all, worried about bills and how to pay them without Dan, worried about somewhere to live with the kids. 'I continued to spend all of my time online with Paul, and Dan continued to not worry about it. I didn't hide my relationship with Paul from Dan but I didn't fully tell him the whole truth either, not at first. I didn't want conflict, I lived with my guilt and that can really mess you up'.

**Hearts Desire, a clicks-and-mortar shop selling virtual shoes for real money.**

Rhonda got messed up all right. Her hair started to fall out, she gained a lot of weight, she ended up in the hospital suffering from anxiety attacks. Then one morning everything changed again. It changed because Paul was crying. He told Rhonda that he didn't think they would ever be together, he didn't think she would ever leave Dan. Paul's heart was breaking, and Rhonda knew he didn't deserve to be feeling like that.

## She logged into a virtual world and met the man she had been dreaming of her entire life

'I broke down and told Dan that day that I had to leave. Dan told me that he thought it was for the best for me to be happy. Dan always knew that it was "Joe" that I loved. . . . '

Rhonda moved back to California the next week, and around the same was contacted by a TV company wanting to make a documentary about the online love affair. Better still, they wanted to fly Rhonda to the UK to meet Paul in person. Heart and Joe, Rhonda and Paul, met for the first time in real life on 19 July 2007, some two and a half years after they got married online. 'We didn't let go of each other for at least a half hour, we kissed and cried and told each other we loved each other. Within hours he had proposed to me at a café on the Thames. I said yes'.

Rhonda was just an average woman in a relationship that was going nowhere slowly. She logged into a virtual world and met the man she had been dreaming of her entire life.

**Nathan and Kelly break the mould with simultaneous real world and virtual marriages.**

Nathan and Kelly did not meet online, nor did the romance blossom there. However, they did decide to get married simultaneously in real life and virtually within the EverQuest II online game environment. Nathan had been playing EverQuest II, a fantasy role playing game set within a 3D virtual world, for 3 years or so. 'Since I started playing EQ2, I've made a lot of good friends, and it satisfies my human desire for social interaction in a healthy manner'. Having asked Kelly to marry him, and having decided to do so while they were in Las Vegas for an EverQuest II fan convention, Nathan opted for an in-character and in-costume wedding. One thing led to another, and before you knew it the idea of the world's first simultaneous in-game and in-real-life wedding was arranged. On Saturday, 4 August 2007, the couple were married, computer screens perched atop the altar so they could control their avatars in-game at the same time as exchanging vows in real life. 'I love the idea that our union will live in cyberspace long after we leave the real world,' Kelly says.

You can buy a wedding dress in There.com but virtual weddings come with no guarantees.

**A jungle pool party is within your reach in the virtual world.**

**The environment can be pure fantasy, but the conversation is real enough.**

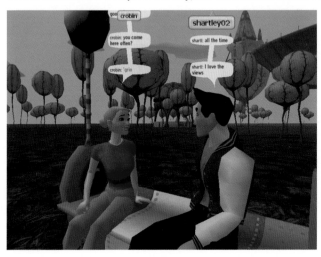

Not all virtual marriages last long enough to cross over into the world of real relationships, as Ronnie found out. He met an avatar girl, they got talking for 9 hours straight, they dreamed of getting married in-world. They also decided a real-world romance would be a bad idea as they lived a few thousand miles apart. Secretly Ronnie wanted to meet up in real life eventually; living together virtually seemed a good first step. Virtual land was purchased, a virtual house was built and the couple got married in a virtual church that Ronnie had also built for the occasion. With the virtual wedding over, reality kicked in.

A few months later, back in the real world, his bride moved to a different city in the USA to live with her grandma who did not have Internet access. The contact and closeness the couple once shared started to slowly slip away. Just seven months after they got married, and before they ever got the chance to meet each other in real life, the couple went their separate ways. Ronnie got kicked out of the marital home, and while both avatars still live on they mix with different people now. Perhaps the virtual and real worlds have something in common after all . . .

# 5  Gender Bending

**Although I was constantly searching** for my identity online, I never seriously looked for it in the guise of the opposite sex. The many personas I experimented with on CIX and the Internet at large were predominantly male. In fact my own experience of gender play was pretty much restricted to the Pythonesque comedy caricature genre, most definitely without any overt sexual undertones. I recall being annoyed with another user for always having to have the last word in a conversation, rather ironically considering my own online behaviour. My solution was to create an account pertaining to be his mother and follow him around the system, posting replies wherever he happened to be to let him know his tea was ready, it was time for bed, to wear clean underpants ... I was obviously not his real mum, and just as obviously not a real woman either. But spotting the gender benders online is not always this straightforward, bizarrely less so now that we have moved away from purely text-based environments and into the age of the avatar. Switching sex is as simple as clicking on the male or female character option when creating the virtual you. When it comes to first impressions there is no easy way to tell the true sexual identity behind the cartoon clothing.

**Switching sex** is as **simple** as **clicking on** the male or **female** character option when **creating** the **virtual you**

I first got to know Steve when I first got to know cyberspace, it is as if he has always been there, hanging around and helping people out. Indeed, if it were not for Steve my first book would never have seen the light of day, as he responded to my online appeal in 1992 when the manuscript needed printing. Trouble was, I had neither a working printer nor the money to buy one that did. Steve turned up a couple of days later, printer in hand. He never asked for any money, he never asked for the printer back.

All he got from me was my respect, and a lifelong friendship.

Steve is typical of the outsider company that I keep, typical of the outsider identities that pepper the online world: salt of the earth but with a twist of citrus. In Steve's case his bit of zest happens to be a fascination with the world of sexual fetish, online and off. It was largely through Steve that I became a regular face at fetish clubs with names such as Whiplash and Submission. Big guys with tattoos, black leather and attitude were typical attendees, but the wheelchair was a pretty unique fashion and fetish accessory even for this crowd. Not that anyone even batted a heavily guyliner-darkened eyelid or raised a pierced brow. I guess that in an environment where it was not unusual for a captain of industry wearing a gimp mask to be led around on a dog lead by a high-heeled if not well-heeled dominatrix, a kinky cyber-cripple does not stand out as strange.

Steve has, funnily enough, become something of an expert when it comes to understanding sexuality and gender online. He was the first person I turned to when trying to get the definitive answer to the question: how do you spot the bloke pretending to be a woman online?

Oddly enough, while it does exist, male role-playing amongst women in virtual environments would appear to be a true minority interest. Neutrality and androgyny are far more common, a defence mechanism to protect the person behind the avatar from unwanted predatory male attention perhaps, but actively taking on the male persona is a rarity in relative terms.

# Male role-playing amongst women in virtual environments would appear to be a true minority interest

'Women, freed from their social framework (mothers, mothers-in-law, coffee mornings) pursue their fantasies in completely different ways to men' says Steve. 'They are less directed, less single-minded, and the fantasies tend to be a lot more continuous. Men achieve orgasm, and then turn into a different person. This directedness shows up even in text-only encounters where men tend to have something in mind that will get them off. Women are much more multi-purpose. When they are in a bad mood, almost anything will stop them whereas men can be in a god-awful mood and they will still make the effort to get off. Also, in general, men use punctuation in chat: women don't'.

Think of identity in terms of the bits we control and the bits we can't control. We like to think that what we say, how we treat people, the atmosphere we create and the topics that interest us are controllable. How we are perceived is usually outside of it. Beyond dieting and exercise, such things as height, voice, age and race are genetically set. Gender falls into the out of our control group, unless you are online. 'Using this in control/out of control model explains a lot of seemingly weird online choices'.

The ability to alter to the one thing they are least genuinely in control of in real life is a powerful drug, and it is little wonder that many people become addicted. Not least because simply by creating a sexy female avatar, the otherwise overlooked male, drowning in a sea of gender similarity, can almost guarantee attention.

The fact that much of this will be overtly sexual in nature, far from putting the gender-bending male off can become one of the attractions. Forget notions of repressed homosexuality; this is a pure power play. The unheard nerd can, at last, gain control over other males. It is the most surreal twist on those old Charles Atlas sand kicked in face adverts from the fifties and sixties. Who would have thought that instead of becoming more masculine and muscular to gain the respect and admiration of the testosterone tribe, what it really needed was to become more feminine?

# Forget notions of repressed homosexuality, this is a pure power play

Brian knows all about being feminine online: he's been doing it for four solid years now with a fair degree of success. No mean feat when you realise that his chosen playground is There.com, a virtual world which allows its users to talk to each other with their real voices. If you are indulging in gender-switching activity, this could be problematical, to say the least. Brian quickly discovered that it is not possible to simply shift the entire audio spectrum using computer technology without bringing an artificial quality to the speech, and so began studying the differences between the way men and women speak.

'Women generally tend to speak with greater modulation, whereas men tend to speak more in a monotone. This is often recognized by men who are trying to sound feminine but a common mistake is to overemphasize one's expressiveness, which tends to result more in sounding like a gay male rather than a woman. One must also pay attention to subtle conversational cues in word choices and phrasing that can influence the listener's perception of gender. I would say it is also linked to one's mindset: it is easier to be convincing as a female by casting oneself in that role rather than as a male pretending to be female'.

**Gender in the virtual world goes way beyond the avatar skin.**

**On the Internet nobody knows if you are a dog, or a man for that matter . . .**

Steve argues that while many people discover a side of themselves online which life would otherwise prevent them from exploring, that side which does bubble to the surface was always there to be discovered in the first place. It is not an invention, it is a revelation. 'If you want to deny what you are, it's just a de-stressing exercise. The vast majority of online dominatrixes seem to be harassed mothers with young kids; they feel a great need to punish some man as a representative of the tribe that landed them with the rug-crawling, poo-making little bastards: so they get very dominant. I don't see any denial there. . . . '

But in most cases gender play is less about denying who we are, and more about accepting it. The Beckham effect has gone a long way to bust the myth that having a feminine side somehow precludes real-man status, but many still find it difficult to display their feminine traits for fear of being cast out of the real-man members club.

Online there is no such fear, no social and cultural restraints, no peer pressure and no real-world consequences to expressing the feminine side of the male psyche. No real-world consequences unless you happen to get caught up in a gender-bending love triangle like Brian, that is . . .

I first encountered Jo Bleaux, an inhabitant of There.com, while researching for someone to talk to about what it is like being an older person in what is often considered a playground for the young and trendy. This 52-year-old grandma had been a resident of the virtual world for 3 years, with plenty to say on what it is like being the tribal elder.

But life, especially virtual life, has a funny way of delivering twists and turns in almost every tale told, and the real Jo Bleaux story had nothing to do with age and everything to do with gender.

Jo was actually a man named Brian, having chosen to represent himself in-world as female in order to escape the dynamics of most online male–female interactions. A plan that would backfire magnificently when a real woman fell in love with him, thinking he was a she.

Brian met Laurie online, in an interactive text-based game known as a MOO, when both had reached breaking point in their respective marriages. The couple quickly found themselves attracted to each other, and Brian travelled from Indiana to Ontario to meet Laurie in person. 'It was love at first sight', says Brian, and Laurie soon packed her bags and moved to Indiana to be with him. They were married in the mid-1990s, but what began as a passionate affair transformed over the rocky passage of years into what Brian describes as being a pragmatic friendship. 'We have come to realise that it is futile to try to recapture the past and wish to no longer inflict injury upon one another with unrealistic expectations, nor hinder each other from finding happiness'. For many years Brian was unaware that a chronic illness was destroying both her health and her libido, and while counselling

**Jo Bleaux is proof positive that first impressions can be deceptive online.**

did help them both to communicate better with each other, it could not restore the desire that had once been there. 'I found it very difficult to not take it personally, but in truth my wife not only did not want me, she simply did not want anyone'.

## MOO

A MOO is a variation of a Multi User Dungeon (MUD) game where multiple users can connect simultaneously and chat in-game. In many ways the MOO was the direct predecessor of the virtual worlds we see today.

Fuelled by hostilities and alienation, their interests and activities took separate paths. While Laurie continued to visit the MOO where the couple had met, Brian took an administrative role on another system. 'I was bored by the former and she felt out of place on the latter. Over the years we had attended numerous real-life gatherings and while I was still interested in going, she began to find them boring'. Part of Brian's interest concerned the fact that some of his friends were in polyamorous relationships, married yet openly spending time with other lovers. Part of Laurie's disinterest concerned the fact that much of the time these gatherings focused on video games, and she just didn't enjoy games that entailed fighting and killing.

## The Sims

The Sims was a ground-breaking computer game in the year 2000, a life simulation where the player took on the role of a member of a virtual household and participated in virtual family life.

With The Sims it was a different story, and Laurie began playing computer games in earnest. Brian had often remarked that it would really be cool if somehow the text-based virtual reality of a MOO could be translated into a visual environment, and it appeared as though that might finally happen with the arrival of The Sims Online. 'We obtained the beta software, but could not get it to install on any of our systems. Then we learned about There.com. I thought perhaps that it might provide an environment where we could spend time together, but I didn't want to be her husband in There.com because my personal situation was just too painful. I did not want to discuss it with anyone, nor did I want to play out the charade of a happy hubby'.

Brian knew of people on various MOOs who had undergone a virtual sex change and it intrigued him to think of how women might interact if he was just another female. 'It occurred to me that I would also probably encounter men who would be interested in me, but that would be easily solved by telling them I was a lesbian'. What Brian didn't allow for were the number of men on a mission to convert lesbians online, nor did he suspect that his gender-swapping role would be so convincing to lesbian or bisexual women. 'I created a female avatar and began working on presenting myself as a female, starting with the easy and obvious stuff such as complaining about men leaving the toilet seat up, asking if my pants made my butt look fat, etc. As time went on, I began to realise that being feminine was something of a more subtle nature. I decided that exposed cleavage would not be a regular part of my wardrobe'.

It **intrigued** him to **think of how** women might **interact** if **he** was **just another female**

But the time spent in There.com with Laurie was short-lived, as she soon left to seek an alternative virtual environment. 'While all of this was going on, my wife and I were in counselling. I had met someone interesting (and interested) on the MOO and so we discussed the possibility of polyamory and open marriage. I believe she was sincere in her efforts to try a new approach, but jealousy and insecurity proved to be too much and she asked me to discontinue my affair shortly after it began. With considerable reluctance, I agreed. I was crushed with a depression that was to last nearly three years'.

Laurie thought maybe she would be able to cope with Brian seeing a sex worker, and he did indeed explore that option. 'I have the utmost respect for a woman who earns her living by trying to care for the sexual needs of others, but my problem ran much deeper than the average sex worker was prepared to deal with. Many men are content to satisfy their physical urges without the emotional entanglement of a relationship, not so with me. No matter how sweetly a sex worker might behave toward me, I felt like it was all in a days work for her and that at the end of that day, she would probably go home to a boyfriend or husband who would be the recipient of her love and affection. I didn't want to be anyone's chore. I wanted a girlfriend. I wanted a lover. I wanted intimacy. In short, I wanted what I had once shared with my wife'.

In their counselling sessions, Brian tried to explain that his complaint was not simply about the infrequency of sexual encounters, but also about the dynamics. 'I think my wife would like to believe that my fibromyalgia was a major factor in our problems. To be sure, chronic pain was a factor, and so were the side effects of my medication, but the central issue was her complete lack of desire. It was painfully evident that she did not want me and that she would much rather get it over with as quickly as possible. Presenting herself to me as an appliance to be used did little to stimulate my interest and nothing to satisfy my emotional craving for a connection'.

Brian was to find that connection with someone he, or rather she, met in There. com about 2 years ago: a bisexual woman who believed that Brian was a lesbian.

'She likes to tell me that I am the woman she fell in love with, and I enjoy telling people that she made a man of me. I would say that my wife is probably relieved. She has commented on occasion that I seem to be happier these days. Despite the absence of a sexual relationship, we have lived our lives together for more than ten years. It would be extremely disruptive and stressful for both of us to change that. Why should we be enemies when we can all be friends?'

> **❝** She likes to **tell me** that **I am** the **woman she fell in love with**, and I enjoy telling people that **she made a man of me** **❞**

Sara is a 47-year-old divorced singer, born and raised just outside of Washington, D.C. Suffering from chronic depression since childhood, Sara took solace in her songwriting and guitar playing, eventually seeking private treatment later in life as mental illness was taboo to her parents. As was coming out. 'Looking back, I think I married in 1991 to avoid coming out. My folks were strict and old fashioned, and I just wasn't going to spring something like that on them in their seventies. The marriage was okay. I love Dave and he was sweet, a quiet, friendly guy. I was usually working either in newspapers, freelancing in graphics, or playing music in local bars. Dave supported my work in music and enjoyed going to gigs and hobnobbing with my musician friends. We had a beer buddy marriage'.

When her father died in 1994 from colon cancer, Sara was sent spiralling back into a deep depression. In 2000, her mother was dying from the same disease and Sara was turning 40. 'One night, while on the computer, I fell out of my chair. One moment I was typing, and the next moment I was looking at the living room from a very odd perspective. My legs were kicking, I was chewing my tongue, and had peed in my pants. I stood up, wandered around, woke Dave and told him I fell down and was confused. He told me to go to bed. I went to the doctor the next day and learned I had a concussion. He sent me to a neurologist and I was put on seizure medications. During this time mom was getting worse'. The marriage was getting worse as well, with Dave and Sara spending ever less time together. 'When mom died I was taking all sorts of strong medication for this epilepsy that I didn't understand, and Dave split. I sank into a pit of depression'.

In 2002 Sara started dating again, but the romance was quashed by the fact that Keith ended up acting as a caregiver more than a lover although the two have remained friends. 'It was Keith who introduced me to There.com. I think Keith was using it as a sort of surrogate to dating. We ended up parting ways when it came to our respective circles of friends, I ended up finding the gay community. I'd come into There.com identifying myself as bisexual and a dyke. I had a reputation for being very outspoken and not taking any crap. In There.com, as in real life, I am not in the least bit feminine'.

**Sara was attracted to Jo Bleaux the female, and fell in love with Brian the man.**

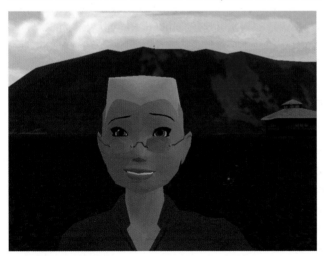

# ❝ In There.com, as in **real life**, **I am not** in the **least** bit feminine ❞

What Sara did not do was enter this virtual world with the intention of dating or even flirting. She was simply looking for new friends at a time when her old life was falling apart and her real-world friends were busy with their music careers or starting families of their own. There.com also offered an escape from depression via activities such as buggy racing, bike racing, house building and even clothes designing. Virtual distraction therapy if you like, and Sara tried most of it. Then her avatar, Dweeb, got hooked on playing the spades card game in-world. 'The spades players tend to be older, and some of the conversation around the table was really hilarious. I got a lot of laugh therapy that way'.

In real life, things were distinctly less amusing.

It was 2005 and the disability pension that Sara had to survive on was just not big enough to keep the apartment that she had once shared with Dave, but was now forced into selling, as he couldn't afford to pay his own rent and contribute to the condo mortgage. 'I was uprooted, but Dave and I split the proceeds and I was able to move away from D.C. to a much cheaper area. In Richmond I was able to buy a modest house, but in a rather dangerous neighbourhood. My There.com friends were pivotal in supporting me through this period and I sought their advice often'.

Sara doesn't remember when she first encountered Jo Bleaux, but Jo was always around the spades players. 'Her voice sounded a bit garbled at times, but she said she had a bad sound card. Jo struck me as being a really intelligent and kind person. She was always helping new people or helping people figure out what was wrong with their computers'. By 2006, with some serious mortgage problems hanging around her neck, Sara found herself increasingly seeking out Jo's soothing personality to talk about her troubles. 'Jo never told me what to do, but always calmed me down and always listened'.

A There.com real-world gathering was planned in August that year, and Sara learned that Jo was going. She decided she wanted to go, too. 'I had a crush on this woman. She was smart, she was funny, she was sweet. I didn't expect a romantic meeting; after all, her profile said she was 51 and in a committed relationship. I figured she was in a rock steady, long-term lesbian relationship. But I wanted to meet her, anyway. I didn't have any lesbian friends my age in Richmond'.

Some of the other spades players were not so sure, they warned Sara that Jo was actually a man. She thought they were just being weird. However, when the time came for the trip Sara chickened out. 'The thought of the crowds, air travel, getting stranded, any number of imagined mishaps, they all dissuaded me from taking the trip. The day of the gathering, I got a phone call from a very male-sounding Jo. I think we were both nervous in that phone call. I was trying to be cool about it, and Jo seemed disappointed that I hadn't come'.

But still the crush remained, and in November 2006 Sara finally plucked up enough courage to say something. She chose a night when Jo, whom she now knew was Brian, had been very quiet while playing spades. When she asked what was wrong Brian replied that he'd had a really bad fight with his wife and bitter words were exchanged.

'He was feeling wounded and worthless. He cried. My heart went out to him and I told him I loved him. Brian didn't approach me because he thought that I was 100% pure lesbian and apparently didn't get the memo that I'm bisexual; I didn't approach Brian because I thought he was an older lesbian in a relationship and wouldn't have time for someone coming out at my age. How funny is that?'

Sara didn't see Jo in There.com for another day or two, finally catching up to finish the conversation they had started. 'He said he was in an open marriage, and I'm pretty sure I actually scoffed at him. He said "Wait a minute, I'll be right back" and left for a minute. He came back and said he'd talked to his wife and she said it was okay. I was blown away. I pulled out my trump card. "Have her call me and tell me herself, and we'll take it from there."'

Laurie called a day or two later, and they talked. 'She gave her blessing. She also suggested we write our needs and expectations and have some guidelines. My biggest guideline was that Laurie's needs and things at home came first. I didn't want Brian dropping everything to come see me if things have to be dealt with at home. Brian made it clear that he was not going to abandon Laurie knowing that she had no means of support and a chronic illness. I respect that most of all'.

Brian and Sara eventually met in real life on New Years Eve 2006 when he travelled up to Richmond to see her. 'I picked him up at the airport, nervous as hell. He didn't say a word as he came up to me. Just walked up, gave me a big hug, and looked into my eyes. He was really there'. Sara and Laurie met the following May, and she suggested Sara move to Indianapolis. 'I thought it was a bit too fast, but looking at my finances in Richmond, I decided to research the idea. The more I learned, the better it looked. I had friends in There.com whose advice played an important role; one woman is a tax accountant, another is a Realtor, and still another is a mortgage broker. I ran over all the numbers with them and with my family. In June of 2007, I bought a modest house outright in a nicer neighbourhood and am now in a position that I can afford to support myself on less than $10,000 a year. Brian and Laurie were fantastic friends while I was selling my house and moving, I lived with them for about a month while the selling and buying negotiations were going on. Laurie gave up the bed for me and slept in her office, but I was uncomfortable with that and stayed in a hotel for the last two or three weeks before I moved into my own place'.

Modern life can be demanding and cold. People hardly have time to pick up milk at the store, they certainly have little time listen to each other apart from yapping on cell phones. It gets harder the older you get, and harder still if you have a disability. 'The three of us are all getting older, we all have our chronic illnesses, we're not close to our families, but we have each other. We hug. We laugh. We encourage each other. It's not about sex. It's about life and love and nurturing. The situation has shown me how narrow-minded people can be. Because Brian was playing a female in There.com people expected that he would be gay, or bisexual, or transexual. Nope. He's just a guy. Because I'm a dyke, people expect that I'm carrying on with his wife as well as him. Nope. Not the case. Laurie is supposed to be jealous, but she's not. I always knew I was different when I was growing up. I figured I'd have a different kind of life. Little did I know how different it would turn out to be'.

Laurie was probably not expecting her life, her role as wife, to turn out quite as it did either. She has been married four times and readily admits that when looking back at her love life over the year she has never exactly been rational. Take her third husband, for example, whom she met at an Elvis impersonation contest. Within the course of a week she had decided to leave her career and her home to move from one side of Canada to the other to be with him. 'After a silly argument somewhere along the line our way of making up was to get married'.

And then there was Brian.

'I was introduced to the Internet and became an all-out addict within weeks of plugging it in. I thought Brian's posts were extremely witty and tended to look for them more and more. We both moved to a text-based game where we could type back and forth in real time and in short order we were professing our undying love for each other. We met after six months of typing and were already making plans for me to uproot myself from my country, my family, my career, to move to the U.S. to live happily ever after with him. I did just that, never once thinking of the consequences'.

The consequences became clear over the course of time when the novelty of living in the USA had faded along with the initial adrenaline rush of being with a new lover. 'Damn, I love that adrenaline rush. I've searched for it in one way or another all my life'.

Brian and Laurie moved from the text-based game environment to the 3D virtual world of There.com, and this was fun for Laurie for maybe a year. Until she discovered that Brian was now Jo the female avatar, and any time they were together became a lesbian by default. 'We very quickly went our separate ways and got different sets of friends'. Eventually they got separate worlds as well, with Laurie jumping ship and settling down in Second Life, where she continues to play today, but not with Brian.

# She discovered that Brian was now Jo the female avatar

**Laurie discovered her husband was pretending to be a woman and had fallen for a lesbian online.**

**If you are having fun, does gender really matter in the virtual world?**

In fact, playing with Brian has always been something of a problem for Laurie. 'Our sex life has never been what I would describe as good. Lack of compatibility, my being on anti-depressants and unbeknownst to me being ill, and the constant pressure I felt to perform all caught up with me. Councillors, books, videos, sex toys, advice from well meaning friends, none of it helped. We fought over this aspect of our relationship until our entire relationship focused on our terrible sex life'.

Then Brian decided he wanted to try polyamory. 'I wanted nothing to do with it as I had no desire to take another lover. So whatever he chose to call it he found himself a friend'.

'I tried to just let it happen but became suicidal. At that point he gave her up. He had the very odd date with prostitutes but that was not fulfilling and it was downright expensive'.

Time passed and both Laurie and Brian became more accepting of where they were in life, and importantly why they were there. Both liked having a roof over their head, transport, food on the table, the trappings of a middle-class life. Divorce was out of the question.

'Brian came to me and brought up the subject of Dweeb, a girl he had met and taken a liking to on There.com. I truly didn't care and that was a surprise to both of us. If he was having sex with another woman it would take the pressure off me and maybe even make him easier to live with. Not to be outdone by me and my snap decisions, Dweeb had moved to the city we live in within a couple of months'.

It turned out that Laurie and Dweeb (Sara) got on quite well. 'When the three of us are together it's a lot of laughs. When she and I are together I enjoy myself. Brian is not nearly so down as he was. I have some precious time alone with my cats and some time with Brian at home. Brian has time alone with Dweeb. We spend time as a trio and I am not the least bit jealous'.

# 6 Age Matters

**This story of a gender**-bending love triangle with all the characters being of 'a certain age' would probably be rejected by most publishers as being too far-fetched, totally unbelievable. Not least because of the age factor, after all, the Internet is the plaything of the young and the older generation are technophobes one and all. At least that is the impression you might get from much of the media coverage given to matters cyber.

The truth, however, paints a completely different picture of Internet usage. One where, according to the UK Communications Market 2007 report (www.ofcom.org. uk/research/cm/cmr07), published by the media regulator Ofcom, silver surfers spend **more** time online than the younger generation. Whereas those in the 18- to 24-year-old age group spent an average of 37.9 hours every month exploring the Web, the figure for over 65s was 42 hours and 80% of that activity is from old men rather than women.

## YouTube

YouTube, owned by Google, is a website which allows anyone to upload video clips which are then viewable by anyone online. Hugely popular, YouTube video clips are viewed more than 100 million times every day.

One 'old man' who has embraced the Web, and who has been embraced right back, is Peter Oakley from Leicester. In August 2006 Peter, using the pseudonym geriatric1927, posted a 2-minute long video clip on YouTube. The video consisted of Peter, a self-confessed grumpy old man of 80, 'bitching and moaning about the world in general from the perspective of an old person who has been there and done that'.

That video has been watched more than 2.6 million times, and in all his video diary has been viewed 6.4 million times and Peter ranks as the twentieth most sub-scribed to YouTube contributor of all time. According to his entry in Wikipedia his fame has truly spread across the Internet. Peter is the 'coolest old dude alive'.

So the Internet is most certainly not the exclusive domain of the young, and not all of the pensioner population is technophobic. Indeed, I conducted a pop quiz amongst elderly neighbours and relatives alike, and of the 50 people I contacted 42 had an email address, 30 had broadband Internet access, 20 used an Internet tele-phone such as Skype to cut down on bills, 18 used a webcam to keep in touch with family and friends abroad and absolutely none had even heard of virtual worlds let alone had a second life in one.

Absolutely **none** had **even heard of virtual worlds** let **alone** had a **second life in one**

I actually thought it quite amusing, when researching for this book, and placing requests within the community notice-boards of virtual worlds for 'silver surfers' who would like to share their virtual experiences, that a number of the people who replied were under 40 years of age.

One typical 35-year-old explained that as he was twice the age of the average in-world resident, he considered himself to be a veteran. More to the point, he assured me that the general avatar population considered him to be the same. He even noted that when chatting with people in-world and mentioning his age, reactions had varied from 'that's cool' to 'get outta here grandad' right up to one female teenage avatar screaming and running away as if he was some kind of pervert.

Interestingly, I suspect that the demographic of your typical virtual world neighbourhood is driven not so much by what is culturally acceptable, but rather by the understanding of and access to suitable technology. Going back to my pop quiz seniors, all but half a dozen were using computers that had either been donated to them by one of the children or grandchildren, or picked up cheaply at a charity shop. Computers that were already past their sell-by date when they got them, which quite frankly would not have the necessary processing power to run the software required to access most virtual worlds. The reason that immersive 3D graphical worlds were not a big thing even 5 or 6 years ago is that the hardware needed to be immersed within them was not generally available outside of academic, corporate and dedicated hobbyist circles. That is the one thing that has changed recently, and a basic family computer these days that will be powerful enough to open the door into that virtual world is affordable for most budgets. Not, perhaps, that of a pensioner on a fixed income, however.

Sally Berry is typical of the older generation of Internet users who see it as a means of communication, a faculty for sharing information about a common interest. As far as Sally, 68, is concerned her virtual identity is an extension of an aspect of her personality and lifestyle, namely her interest in allotments. Sally is the force behind the longest running online community of allotment users in the UK, the popular Allotments-UK website (www.allotments-uk.com). An allotment owner for 35 years, she launched the site in 2004 and it now has an active membership of more than 3000 people.

**Sally Berry is typical of the older generation embracing the Internet.**

With maps of allotment locations around the country that link to their owners' blogs, helpful articles and advice forums, even its own web-based TV channel Sally is certainly kept busy. So what drives her? 'In the case of a community site based on life style like allotments, the internet is actually an opportunity to look further into yourself and your passion. In real life you might not be encouraged to talk about an interest for a long period of time, but online you can look for people who want to hear you views on that subject. I'm a gardening enthusiast with a strong interest in family. Allotments at home is a chance to socialise with my family, but online to socialise with friends and allotment aficionados. Although I think both offline and online reveal the maternal element to my personality, I look after my family and I look after my website, I like watching both grow'.

She also likes to think that the virtual world is not turning the real thing into a planet populated by impersonal, unsociable loners. 'I have watched the impact of New Media on the world. From the common use of the telephone to the television, with every new form of communication there will be concerns about it being impersonal. In modern society, with longer working hours it is possible to retire with few friends and no easy way of making new ones. The internet is a way of keeping in contact with people, and making new friends through common interests. If anything we are now communicating more not less'.

Sally is also dismissive of their being any kind of hostility towards older people who establish a virtual presence, arguing that she gets a friendlier reception online than she would if she walked into a pub. 'The internet takes that first judgement away. So it's a more accepting environment where people are represented by their actions and words, not by their grey hair, which is actually quite nice. Not being judged by my cover does give me a certain freedom, and I think that's the same for everybody online whether you'd be judged on age, hair colour, gender, or race'.

# ❝❝ **People** are represented by **their actions** and **words**, **not** by **their grey hair** ❞❞

When it comes to the other end of the age scale, kids are well versed in every aspect of technology, from mobile phones to DVD recorders. The Internet is as much a part of their world as telephones and television were to the generations before. When it comes to virtual worlds for kids, Disney Club Penguin (www. clubpenguin.com) enjoys the highest profile. Aimed specifically at 6- to 14-year-olds, it offers kids the chance to discover a safe virtual world in the guise of a cartoon penguin. The penguins can be dressed up, igloos are created for them to live in, and of course that snow-covered world for the penguins to explore.

Managing to stay advertising-free courtesy of charging a monthly subscription fee for the privilege of being able to dress up your penguin in different clothes and decorate your igloo, Club Penguin attracts some 700,000 subscribing penguins. But that is just the tip of this kiddie iceberg, as there are another 12 million users happy with their free accounts. In fact, according to an article published in *Business Week* (www.businessweek.com/technology/content/may2007/tc20070522_380944.htm) during May 2007, Club Penguin gets a greater share of Web traffic than Second Life and World of Warcraft put together!

But Disney does not have the younger-generation playing field entirely to itself. Snapping at its heels with more than 10 million members, and a unique selling point, is Stardoll (www.stardoll.com), aimed squarely at 7- to 17-year-old girls. It is more social networking with avatars than a totally immersive virtual world though. Indeed, the avatars are a vital component to Stardoll, because they allow young girls to dress them up in much the same way they would any doll, the difference being that online these are their MeDoll identities.

As well as dressing up in the latest fashions and chatting with other members, the MeDolls get the chance to feature as a cover girl on the Stardoll magazine and win cash prizes to be spent on more clothes and accessories in-world. It's nice to find somewhere that bucks the trend and applies a modern twist to both dressing up and playing with dolls. Both of which form an essential part of discovering, through fashion, make-up and role play, who you want to be and who you really are for young girls.

**A Stardoll magazine cover.**

Stardoll all started as the hobby of a Scandinavian-born woman called Liisa. Inspired by a childhood passion for paper dolls, the type you would cut out and dress in paper clothes, she started paperdollheaven.com, where her own celebrity doll designs could be found. With a desire to get away from the violence and competitiveness she saw all around her online, the site was meant as a positive environment for creative young girls. Eventually this became Stardoll, and Liisa still creates new doll designs and uploads them every week.

'Her idea is a global traditional girls' game translated to the possibilities of modern technology', Malin Ströman, Product Manager at Stardoll explains. 'It was natural to develop this idea further to a virtual world for girls as there have been lots of high-quality content for boys on the Internet, but very little pure girls' content of the same high quality. There is children's stuff, news, dating sites and so on, but no meeting place for girls built on their primary interests'. Nobody can argue that fashion and celebrity are high up the list of most girls' interests, although there has been some debate over what is the right age for kids to enter the world of virtual identity and to immerse themselves online within it.

'To develop a virtual identity you need to be able to communicate it to others, and most important, get responses on it from them. The need, and thereby maybe a proper age, for creating a virtual identity I would say will arise at the same time as the tween/teenager starts to collaborate and experiment with their real life identity in relation to the separation from the parents or nearest surrounding environment. This development of a very own, independent, free being of course varies for different people, but could maybe be generalized as the ages of 10 to 14'.

**▌▌ To develop a virtual identity you need to be able to communicate it to others ▌▌**

In the virtual world there are no age limits on having fun.

As we have already discovered through the experiences of Sarah (KiBe), recounted earlier in this book, the Internet can be a more accommodating place than the school yard or the neighbourhood streets to experiment with differing character-istics as we are going through puberty. However, there is no doubting it can also be a dangerous place for young girls to be wandering through alone.

Malin is keen to stress that Stardoll works hard to ensure that it **is** a safe environ-ment. 'Stardoll gets thousands of reports from users every day, and the support teams work around the clock to act upon **every** report that same day. All users' comments go through a constantly updated language filter to remove language that we on Stardoll, parents and users, find improper'.

So what are the benefits of virtual interaction for the kids who participate in the Stardoll experience exactly? What are the positives that they bring away from the dressing up of dolls on a screen? It seems that much of the appeal of Stardoll is actually less to do with social networking or community as such, and more to do with virtual celebrity.

'Stardoll is a virtual substitute to the real celebrity world where most teenagers have no chance to become famous. At some point of life, it is many girls' dreams to be on the cover of some magazine, buy fancy clothes, be a writer or be in the same scene as their favourite celebrities and at Stardoll they can'. It is a place where they can achieve that elusive 15 minutes of fame by appearing on the cover of Stardoll Magazine. Or rather getting their avatar, their MeDoll, to feature.

But it does go beyond a shallow craving to be part of the celebrity culture that has gripped so many otherwise intelligent and civilised nations. In order to attain that virtual celebrity status within Stardoll, its users have to put in the time. There is a real work ethic involved with promoting the MeDoll, creating the character in the first place, giving it a compelling back story to grab attention, organising competitions, listings, composing virtual diaries. This is that good old-fashioned pastime of creative play, it is firing the imagination of young girls once more, and helping them to discover how to be who they want to be through the social interaction with others.

# II  Being There

**Immersive 3D worlds are just** that, totally absorbing, all encompassing and highly addictive places to be. Yet some people not only visit occasionally, they pretty much live their lives within a virtual paradise. Escaping the problems of the real world, an avatar identity can find fame and fortune online. However, as advancing technological development continues to improve the 'being there' experience, what effect can this have on real-world relationships?

**There.com brings a whole new world of possibility into otherwise ordinary lives.**

# 7 Virtual Worlds, Real Lives

**In 1996 an ambitious project** called 24 Hours in Cyberspace, headed up by celebrated photographer Rick Smolan, became the largest Internet collaborative event of its time. Thousands of photographers the world over took pictures of people whose lives had been impacted in some way by the Internet. The images being uploaded to a long since defunct website to create a snapshot of Internet life across a single day. The website was viewed more than 4 million times in that 24 hours, and this 12 years ago when the Internet had yet to make its mark on the media consciousness as it has today. The website became a coffee-table book containing 200 photographs and accompanying stories from the 200,000 that appeared online. One of those stories was about the 'punk leader of London's underground cyber-culture', a chap by the name of Wavey Davey. I was used to these desperate attempts at compartmentalising my identity, putting my personality into a box with a label where it was safe. But whether you believed that I was indeed 'the Barbara Cartland of Cyberspace' as one UK newspaper described me, or the UK's 'first virtual celebrity' as another proudly proclaimed, really didn't matter to me then, or now. I can relate to the concept of self as a paper doll, a plaything to be shaped and coloured as the moment requires, and discarded, crumpled and torn, when that moment passes. Of course, the author of my many adventures in virtual infamy and descents into real-world hell was none other than me, myself and I.

# I can relate to the concept of self as a paper doll

I fed the reporter that Barbara Cartland line, backed up by my having seen 11 books about the Internet published in a 2-year period, which apparently made me the most prolific author of Internet-related books in the world at the time. I didn't do it to massage my ego; I did it because I had a twelfth book to sell. The virtual celebrity thing was pure self-promotion, again to sell a book. I was nothing if not consistent.

In 1994 I had met and fallen in love with Yvonne, a classically trained former ballerina. We married in 1995, but not before I dragged myself out of that wheelchair so that I could make good the promise I had made to myself to walk (albeit with the help of a stick) down the aisle. The wheelchair might have gone, but Wavey Davey remained. The odd, anarchic but strangely compelling cyberspace character had escaped into the real world and was to dominate my personality for the next few years. The punk look did not hinder my career; if anything it helped. After all, who better to present a new series about the Internet for the BBC than someone who not only knew his stuff and was not shy about telling everyone, but who happened to look like something out of a comic book? Who better to appear as an extra in the Judge Dredd movie?

I had the chance that so many are denied, the chance to be reborn. Not in a spiritual or religious sense, although I did discover an empathy with paganism that remains to this day. What I really mean is that I was born again, the real me. I did not regain a lost identity, even if long buried parts of my personality did make the odd appearance every now and then. I created an entirely new one.

## I did not **regain** a **lost identity**, I created an **entirely new one**

Fast-forward a decade and creating new lives online has become something of an obsession with millions of people the world over. According to Internet World Stats (www.internetworldstats.com), which provide an accurate reflection of the online population, as of July 2007 there are some 1,173,109,925 people who use the Internet across the globe. In March 2007, Point Topic (www.point-topic.com) estimated 300 million of them were accessing it via broadband, 14 million of them in the UK alone. Now this is, perhaps, the most important statistic of all, because it means that increasingly we have cheap and easy access to audio and video connections. It means that online communication is moving away from being a flat textual experience and becoming a much richer, multimedia thing. Virtual worlds are no longer the plaything of the fortunate few with their university or corporate fat pipe connections: now anyone can join in.

## **There are** some 1,173,109,925 **people** who use the **Internet across the globe**

And that's exactly what they are doing.

We have pretty much hit a tipping point in social interaction and networking that takes communication to a whole new level of connectivity. So much so that if we, for whatever reason, try and sever that communication we soon discover that it is actually all but impossible.

The very infrastructure of the Internet was built around the basic assertion that the network interprets censorship as damage and routes around it. Remove one section of the network and data finds another route to its ultimate destination, in other words. The communication will always be completed, and so it is with the relationships we build online, one connected to the other, in such a way that if we try and take ourselves out of the loop we soon discover it catches back up with us at some point.

The whole six degrees of separation thing kicks into effect.

An experiment undertaken at the Columbia University in New York back in 2003 sought to prove the theory that everyone in the world can be linked by six social ties. It used 60,000 volunteers from 166 different countries around the world, and asked them to contact one of 18 randomly chosen target people (an American scholar, a Norwegian Vet and so on) by sending an email to someone they already knew. That person was then asked to send an email to someone they knew who might be more likely to know the target, and so on.

The researchers discovered that on average it took between five and seven email hops to reach the right person, close enough to six degrees for me. With the advent of hugely popular social networks such as Facebook, MySpace and Linked-In it would not surprise me in the least, were this experiment to be repeated, to find it is even easier to reach that unknown target now. And that is both a blessing and a curse because we all need somewhere to run and hide and be alone. The new age of virtual relationships and social connectivity shines a light into even the darkest corners of our lives and reduces the opportunity to escape.

# Social **connectivity shines a light** into **even the darkest corners** of our lives and **reduces the opportunity** to **escape**

Some people give up even trying, and perform the most intimate and personal of acts within the full gaze of an online audience. People like Kevin Whitrick, believed to be the first British man to broadcast his own suicide online by way of a webcam feed into an Internet chat room in March 2007.

Whitrick, 42, logged into a chat room where users went with the specific purpose of insulting each other. The depressed father of two had recently split from his wife and had also lost his father. He told the gathered chat room users what he was about to do, and while some contacted the police, others goaded him on with insults. This type of behaviour, which few of us could conceive of in a face-to-face situation where most would try to prevent a suicide if we saw one, illustrates that there remains a disassociation between reality and the virtual world, no matter how hard we try to link one to the other.

## There remains a **disassociation between reality** and the **virtual world**

It is not the first time that someone has been helped to take their life online, back in January 2003 Brandon Vedas, a 22-year-old American, consumed vast quantities of prescription and illegal drugs on camera in a chat room. Despite this being a case of foolish drug-ridden bravado rather than intended suicide, it does further illustrate the separation between reality and virtuality. Before taking the final batch of drugs that would prove fatal, Vedas told the onlookers that should anything go wrong they could give the police his car registration details as it was parked outside his house and they would find him quickly enough. Once he had collapsed, nobody called the police for fear of involving Vedas and themselves in an investigation. His brother, on the site he maintains as a memorial to Brandon, writes 'whether in person or online, we as humankind are given the task of looking out for those we care about'.

Thankfully, this task, this basic human quest of kindness and compassion, has found a home online within the virtual worlds that so many are quick to dismiss as nothing more than a game for geeks. People are forming disembodied relationships within imaginary places, relationships and places as important to them as any made of flesh and stone. We have already heard how people have fallen in love, have found a freedom from the real-world disabilities that life had dealt them, and in the case of Buddy, how a virtual world has provided a very real lifeline for his future care.

Jeff has also felt the full force of empowerment that virtual life can bring.

Suffering from an anxiety disorder brought on by years of working in a high-stress occupation, he found himself unable to 'let go' when anything made him angry or scared. His body would just keep on pumping that adrenalin, and pumping it in massive amounts, sometimes for hours at a time. 'Where a normal person can let go of something that has made them angry, or scared, my body keeps producing adrenalin at those times in massive amounts, sometimes for hours at a time. I can still think clearly, I just can't get my body to stop running at a million miles an hour'.

Not the greatest condition to be in if you want to hold down a job where you have a boss to answer to, targets to meet and co-workers to let down every time you have

to run away from the office to escape the stress. Jeff desperately needed to find the kind of work where he could step away for an hour or two when things got too much, where he could function in a near-normal working way without the shackles of a nine-to-five regime.

He found it within the virtual world of There.com.

'My online business started when I found out that members of this virtual world could submit and sell their own dune-buggies and clothing designs. At the time, that's all that was available, but being a kind of hot-rod guy to begin with, I couldn't resist the idea of slapping a few flames or tribal designs on something I could drive around. I painted up a couple of designs, and then made up a black and white tribal one. Once it was approved by There Inc, I started selling it as a limited edition'. Jeff, or rather, Grimm, his in-world avatar, sold 11 of them. Cartel Kustoms, as it

**If you want to travel around There.com in style, chances are it will be in a Cartel Kustoms creation.**

is known in There.com, did not really start making money for about a year or so, but it did enough in-world money to be able to submit more items, and build up an inventory.

> ❚❚ Being **able to work** in a virtual world has
> **literally** saved me from the gutter ❚❚

Jeff soon diversified into clothing, and also tried his hand at some complex hover-bike designs, buggies and hoverboats as means of virtual transportation. 'About two years ago I started making enough to actually make an impact in the real world. Now, I pull in enough every month to help with all of the household bills enough to consider this a job, which comes in pretty handy seeing as my condition prevents me from attempting any normal 9–5 routine. Being able to work in a virtual world has literally saved me from the gutter'.

## Virtual Economy

Although it can be hard to get your head around the concept of a totally virtual economy, where people can attain a status equivalent to that of the A-list celebrity in terms of wealth and fame, that is just what is happening online. As the population of any virtual world expands, so the demand for land, property, clothing, transportation and even services grows. Exactly what is available to purchase will vary from system to system. Some such as Second Life allow its residents to create pretty much anything and everything, just retaining control over the initial sale and servicing of land. Others, such as There.com, keep a firmer hand on what content is user-creatable.

One virtual resident who certainly is making enough in-world money to live on would be Anshe Chung, a property developer who has appeared on the cover of *Business Week* magazine, who has made a million dollars in less than 3 years, and who just so happens to be an avatar. The first person to make a million dollars running a business entirely within the confines of a virtual world, Anshe Chung has built a portfolio in Second Life that includes a number of shopping malls, high street store chains, real estate equivalent to some 40 square kilometres of land, and cash holdings of several million Linden Dollars. Not bad for an initial investment of just ten dollars by the woman behind the avatar, Chinese-born German citizen Ailin Graef. In fact, virtual business is so good that Graef is now CEO of Anshe Chung Studios (www.anshechung.com) with offices in China and a real-world staff in excess of 60, developing immersive 3D environments.

## Ailin Graef's avatar, Anshe Chung, is the first person to make a million dollars running a business entirely within the confines of a virtual world

The virtual world is not just about making money or building a new life. Michael Wilson, the CEO of There.com, which has more than a million active members, likes to think that it's also about building a richer form of interaction. 'Richer than email and text-IM, certainly, but also richer than social networks like Facebook and MySpace'. There.com doesn't replace those mediums, but it does provide an option to express yourself in an entirely different way via your 3D avatar. 'Your range of expression then goes from the 2D to a 3D virtual space where you can chat, emote, change your appearance, change your clothing, participate in activities (including competitive kinetic sports), make things (clothing, vehicles, homes, etc.) and even become your own virtual brand'.

Defining a virtual world as a space where you can represent yourself in whatever form you like, communicate and build relationships with other residents and even participate in physical activities such as sports or dancing, Michael is quick to counter the argument that such immersion within a fantasy world is a bad thing.

**There.com Michael Wilson as he appears in-world.**

IMAGE COURTESY OF THERE.COM

'We certainly don't want people to spend their life in There.com, or any other virtual environment, but we would like There to become part, or an extension if you will, of our members' lives. I believe we will use the virtual self as an extension to our communications with others. In the end, the quality communications, the ones that count, will be an extension of us, even if they don't (on the surface) match our in-person view. In the end, I believe that the persona we reflect in the online world is an actual reflection of our real persona whether we intend it to be or not'.

Increasingly, however, people **are** investigating ways maybe not to escape from the realities of life, but to solve the problems those realities bring with them. A chance to replace a seemingly hopeless existence with a meaningful one, to look into the mirror and see something less desperate staring back. One such virtual resident looking for some virtual salvation is 48-year-old Mark from Florida.

Laid off from IBM in 1995 after 13 years of service, Mark spent 6 years travelling around the USA working as a printed circuit board designer. Things were going remarkably well. Losing that IBM 'job for life' wasn't, perhaps, the disaster Mark had at first thought. As a PCB designer he had to deal with highly technical issues of component placement and trace routing, an extremely intense and focussed process of figuring out how to get from point to point.

'I would tell people I spend my day working my way through a maze. It kept my mind highly engaged and active'. On the morning of 11 September 2001, Mark watched in shock as the events of that day started to unfold before him on the television news. Little did he realise quite precisely how that terrorist attack would rebound upon his life.

'There was a dramatic drop in contracting positions as well as all forms of employment that followed. The longest I had been unemployed was no more than three months, but I had some money in the bank and equity in my home, so I was pre-pared to hold on for more than the recommended six months of unemployment that had always been the rule of thumb'.

After a year Mark started worrying that he was losing his technical vitality in the design business, as well as losing touch with the expensive software tools of the trade. After 2 years of unemployment he was worrying about paying his bills and keeping his medical insurance.

After 3 years his worries proved to be correct, and Mark lost both his health cover-age and his ability to meet his monthly payments. 'I fell into economic ruin after 9/11 and spent 3 years 9 months trying to find employment, during which time I lost all my savings, my home and my van. Finally, at the end of May 2005, I was able to secure a job taking incoming phone calls for entry into a sweepstakes and then determine if they had a debit/credit card and attempt to sell them magazine sub-scriptions. I was making less in three weeks than I had made in one day when last doing PCB design work'. Mark left that job after 2 months, working part time where he could and ending up struggling to find anything full time that could offer anything suited to his skills and experience.

At 48 years old and living in a studio apartment with just his cat as company, Mark realised that all he had worked hard to achieve, all that he was, had slipped between his fingers like so many grains of sand. It was only natural, given the cir-cumstances, to fall into a pit of depression. 'I guess I still haven't hit rock bottom yet, but I'm close to it now'.

Mark knew that without health insurance he could not afford to get the medical attention he needed to treat his depression. An educated man, one of his degrees being in Social and Behavioural Sciences, Mark sought out an alternative, a means to redirect himself and, he hoped, take his mind off his myriad problems. Mark discovered There.com.

'There.com offered me a means to socialize with others again. I got to meet a broad spectrum of people: young to old, begging kids to folks with money to burn, and those who you can have an enjoyable time with just chatting and debating issues of the day. I've met so many talented people from around the world and in doing so I found a wealth that I doubt I will ever regain in real life. Maybe virtual reality is the opium of the intellectuals, but in the end friends are the family we get to choose'.

Mark also discovered the benefits of an in-world economy by designing content which can be sold to the highest bidder through the There.com auction system. 'I found that There.com let me regain, if only virtually, the status of a productive person. Someone who is respected for the ability to create new content in our world. Creating designs in There.com lets me maintain my design ability and create new challenges'.

**❛❛ There.com let me regain,** if only **virtually,** the status of a **productive person ❜❜**

With enough items being sold in auction, and therefore being used by residents of the virtual world, a certain dignity can be reclaimed by way of building a reputation. 'It always pleases me to come upon my creations in world and to see how folks have made use of them and to be recognized by these strangers and fawned over is a pleasant stroke of your ego. If only it was this easy in the real world, I'm telling you!'

Mark doesn't make enough money to quit his part-time job, he doesn't create the kind of income you can live off, although there are increasingly more people who

Everyone has a voice online.

IMAGE COURTESY OF THERE.COM

The world might be virtual, but There.com provides a real sense of belonging for its members.

IMAGE COURTESY OF THERE.COM

are achieving just that. But when he was recently faced with a car repair bill and had no cash to pay it, Mark could exchange some of his in-world wealth for real world dollars and pay off the $200 that was owed.

'I may not make a lot in sales, but I take pride in myself and my work. I feel more worthy and it helps me keep my life in perspective. It gives me hope that things can get better. After all, if I still have it THERE then I should still be able to have it HERE. You may lose your faith and charity, but never give up hope'.

**❝ If I still have it THERE then I should still be able to have it HERE ❞**

# 8 Social Networks and Second Lives

**It is not just within** the graphically believable worlds of avatars and adventure that new friendships are made and old ones rediscovered. Fantastically flat two dimensional environments can be just as absorbing, just as addictive. While I would argue that a virtual community is just that, no matter what trendy tag might be attached, and can stretch right back to those FidoNet bulletin boards I used to frequent before many of the inhabitants of There.com or Second Life were even born, there is no denying that as technology moves on, so the nature of that community building moves with it.

Nowhere is this more apparent in the Web 2.0-driven ideal of the social networking sites.

## Web 2.0

Web 2.0 is either the future of the Internet or nothing more than media-friendly jargon used to over-inflate the market value of Internet companies in some kind of sequel to the dotcom revolution. None other than Stephen Fry is quoted (www.videojug.com/interview/stephen-fry-web-20) as saying that it is 'an idea in people's heads rather than a reality'. However, if you think of it as encompassing Web-based services promoting collaboration and sharing between users, you are not far wrong. Everything from blogging to podcasts to YouTube and social networking sites can be found under the Web 2.0 umbrella.

## Social Networking

Social networking sites do pretty much what it says on the tin: they allow people to create networks of friends, reach out to the friends of those friends, and generally keep everyone updated with every facet of their lives.

Be it the likes of MySpace (www.myspace.com), which has helped launch the music careers of Lily Allen and the Arctic Monkeys, or the business-oriented LinkedIn (www.linkedin.com), which moves the old boys' network firmly into the twenty-first century, these social sites have taken the concept of virtual community to a whole new level. Want an idea of just how obsessed we are becoming with social networking? How about the 1 billion minutes a month spent online at

Facebook (www.facebook.com) by its 60 million members worldwide? The idea is compelling enough: post a potted biography of yourself, search for friends you already know who may be using Facebook already and then sit back and wait for your social circle to grow. The friend-of-a-friend concept is particularly attractive because it appeals to our almost universal desire to know and be known. Whereas we might make friends with our friends' mates in the pub or club, most of us would not call all the contacts on their mobile phone and introduce ourselves in the off chance that they were looking for a new chum. Yet that is exactly what happens online within a social networking context, and nobody seems to mind. Nobody seems to question the true value of these Facebook friendships either. Many people treat social networking as some kind of game. They are on a quest to collect friends, the prize for getting 350 mates being to feel better than you did when you only had 349.

## Many people treat **social networking** as **some kind of game**

Recent research by Dr Will Reader at Sheffield Hallam University suggests that while people will claim to have more friends than ever, collecting Facebook friends is no guarantee that in the real world you are not Billy No-Mates. Dr Reader concluded that no matter how many friends we collect in this way, the real-life close friend count always remains pretty constant. However, I'm not at all convinced that this really matters. After all, what is the benefit of creating a distinction between the friends we drink a pint with at the pub or share a conversation with at work and those we chat to online or hang out with in avatar form? Is a friend not a friend regardless of where the friendship is forged, irrespective of how the friendship is maintained?

# Collecting **Facebook friends** is **no guarantee** that **in the real world** you **are not** Billy **No-Mates**

Catherine Smith, Director of Marketing and Brand Strategy at Linden Lab, the company behind Second Life, would seem to agree. 'With the advent of virtual worlds and social media sites, the world has become smaller. Online communities now exist that share interests and experiences. They have brought together a group of people who would not normally have connected. Today, we live in a world without boundaries, we can talk with someone in Japan and Australia as easily as someone in our own back garden, distance is no longer an issue and virtual worlds only enhance shared experience'.

The notion of a collective shared experience is key to the success of community in the Web 2.0 world of social networking and second lives. Yet psychologists have insisted for the longest time that certain social rules are part and parcel of our genetic make-up and there is little we can do to change that, even by entering a virtual world such as Second Life.

In his concisely titled paper 'The Unbearable Likeness of Being Digital: The Persistence of Nonverbal Social Norms in Online Virtual Environments' (pdf file at www.nickyee.com/cv.html) Stanford University graduate Nick Yee claims 'our findings support our overall hypothesis that our social interactions in online virtual environments, such as Second Life, are governed by the same social norms as social interactions in the physical world'. He goes on in some detail to explain how a study revealed that just as women have a tendency to stand closer together during a conversation than men, and men are less likely to maintain eye contact, avatars in Second Life showed exactly the same behavioural tendencies. Even more fascinating, the study of 1600 avatar interactions revealed that when one avatar gets within a few metres of another, eye contact is reduced by moving the avatar so that it does not face the other directly.

The study of 1600 avatar **interactions revealed that** when one **avatar** gets within a **few metres** of another, **eye contact is reduced**

Of course, quite how much of this avatar interaction is under the direct control of the person in front of the computer screen, and how much is scripted behaviour buried deep within the user interface code behind the Second Life program remains unclear.

It is this lack of clarity that troubles many observers when looking at the direction that some people are pushing their social network usage. Take the strange case of Lonelygirl15 (www.youtube.com/profile?user=lonelygirl15), a video diary of a teenager on the run which captivated the YouTube audience when it first appeared in May 2006. So much so, in fact, that it went on to become the second most sub-scribed to series of video in YouTube history, with an average of 300,000 views per 'episode' and a total viewing figure in excess of 60 million.

Not bad for a teenage girl on the run.

But if you are thinking that all this talk of episodes and viewing figures has a ring of television to it, you would be right. Lonelygirl15 was a soap opera for the

YouTube generation, carefully conceived by three twenty-somethings from California. It was TV through and through, right down to the commercial product placement advertising – another first for YouTube. The same production team eventually moved the concept off of the video-sharing stage and directly into the social networking environment with KateModern to be broadcast on BeBo.

# Lonelygirl15 was a **soap opera** for the YouTube **generation**

## Bebo

Bebo (www.bebo.com) is a social networking site with 35 million members worldwide that allows for all the usual photo sharing, profile making, conversation facilitating you would expect.

KateModern follows the Lonelygirl15 lead by being a series of video episodes which are published on YouTube, but directly links the characters in the cyber-soap with their Bebo profiles. This means that viewers of the story can actually influence the plot line week on week by interacting with the 'people' behind the profiles, the characters in the soap.

Ironically the drama revolves around the story of four young adults searching for their personal identity across the Internet and through the streets of London simultaneously. The Kate in question is a 20-year-old university art student struggling to balance her complex social life with the dark forces that shadow her. All typical and harmless soap opera fare you might think, and you might be right. However, in a celebrity-obsessed youth culture one has to air a certain degree of caution over enabling impressionable youngsters to get sucked into a heady mix of soap stars and social belonging. If social networking is meant to provide a route to relationship building, a communications channel with an expanded circle of con-tacts, I find it hard to figure out exactly where this kind of fantasy fits in.

Imaginary friends were never as real as this when I was a lad . . .

# III Game Over

**It would be easy to** imagine that virtual worlds are places conjured up from your dreams, but they can also be nightmarish visions if you allow them. When identity confusion sets in, when the real and virtual collide, that's when the problems start. Whether it is being addicted to virtual murder or virtual sex, or thinking that real-world laws do not apply in virtual spaces, facing up to the real-world consequences of online actions can be a tough call to make.

**Virtual worlds can involve conflict as well as conversation.**

# 9 Addicted to Murder

**I recall during one particularly** dark moment in my life, with the black dog of depression sitting heavily upon my chest, when I asked one of my online friends if he could arrange my murder. This is probably not the kind of thing that would crop up in most real-world conversations, yet it seemed a perfectly natural question to ask with the virtual safety net of the virtual environment beneath me. My friend, being just that, not only dismissed the idea but managed to talk me through my suicidal thoughts and out the other side back into the well-lit, and dogless, day of normality.

I asked one of **my online friends** if **he** could **arrange my murder**

The point being that although I did not realise it at the time, there was no virtual safety net. In fact, if anything, it would be less risky to enter into an arrangement in the real-world where whispers and meetings might, if you were lucky and had not got caught in some kind of law enforcement sting, go unnoticed.

Online your every movement is recorded, your digital footprints leaving a muddy trail through your murky adventures. Murder is not something you would get away with online, unless you had a virtual victim in mind of course.

Many of us get wrapped up in the fantasy violence of the video game, the murder spree with no consequence as most teenagers today would consider it. You can almost imagine the disclaimer 'no real people were hurt during the playing of this game'.

Where is the harm in taking out the bad guy if that bad guy is comprised entirely of computer console code?

Conversely, as many teenagers are discovering following years of exposure to this comic book killing, where is the fun in it? Head to head multiplayer gaming helped with the dynamics of video gaming death in that at least the opponent was no longer a computer-controlled entity, but one with your mate at the joystick. But after a while, even this cannot sharpen the dullness of the predictability of your prey: fresh meat is what any predator requires and that includes the virtual one. The Internet came to the rescue, along with the availability and affordability of broadband access, to launch multiplayer games into the online realm.

## Virtual Murder Gangs

The most popular MMORPG is World of Warcraft, with more than 9 million players across the globe. Only the bravest, or most foolhardy, avatar would even consider questing in certain regions of the map though. For in the dark corners, the remote wastelands, of this virtual world there exist organised murder gangs. Avatar assassins roaming in search of hapless newbies, easy fodder to be 'killed' and the virtual belongings looted so as to be sold to the highest bidder in return for gold. In-game gold that can then be traded on one of the many black-market game gold exchanges for real cash.

With the added element of the unknown introduced into play, now it was kill or be killed, now the innocent looking avatar you are sneaking up upon could actually be an accomplished assassin just waiting for you to get close enough. Through the medium of the massively multiplayer online role playing game, thankfully reduced to MMORPG amongst aficionados, excitement had returned to the killing genre.

Some people encountered that excitement a decade ago. Some people encountered the addiction to virtual murder long before it became fashionable.

One of them was Richard.

Richard first bumped heads with MUDs and murder back in 1997 as a shy 15-year-old who couldn't help wonder what all the fuss surrounding these strange little online text games was all about. What could possibly be the attraction of a world built on words to a teenager brought up in a world of graphical video gaming? However, it certainly didn't take long for him to become totally immersed in the fantasy, absorbed by the role play and addicted to the virtual life within a MUD.

Addicted to virtual murder.

Richard first began playing MUD as an eager achiever and explorer, quickly making friends and helping those in need, in-world. 'I'd spend my wood-work lessons meticulously redrawing maps of the land from memory. Then, of an evening, I'd get home and wait impatiently until 6pm for off-peak play to begin'.

Remember, 10 years ago there were no all-you-can-eat broadband Internet tariffs, only dial-up modems with very real-world telephone charges attached. This par-

## A (Very) Brief History of MUD

The first MUD, or Multi-User Dungeon, is generally thought to date back to the late seventies and could be found at the University of Essex. Created by Roy Trubshaw and Richard Bartle, this was a multiplayer computer game that brought together the best and worst of board-based role playing games, hack-and-slash computer games and the burgeoning online BBS chat room scene of the age. Think of an online virtual world built entirely out of words and you are pretty much there. Indeed, MUDs that eschewed the game-playing element altogether soon emerged, these entirely social-oriented environments became known as MOOs instead (although I will spare you the mind-numbingly technical explanation of that particular acronym).

ticular MUD, a MUD2 world, brought with it an element of danger. In this game your character could die and there was no bringing it back. 'It's this factor which allows MUD2 to excite the same areas of my brain as rock climbing and skiing does. Living on the edge one false move from death'. This might sound fantastical to anyone who has never delved within an online world of any sort, but that is entirely the point. It is fantasy, an all-embracing, totally immersive mental and spiritual existence that becomes as real as anything you can reach out and touch physically.

Ironically, being a text-based adventure, the fantasy takes on a much deeper sense of reality than most modern console gamers can experience. Comparing the two gaming genres is like comparing a book with the Hollywood movie version of it. The story that you illustrate with your imagination, that you bring to life through nothing more than your own creative thoughts, is always going to be more immersive and more real than the one someone else paints for you.

There is a reason they are called role-playing games, and for many people the role that is adopted is shaped entirely by in-world experience. A weird blurring of real experiences learned within a virtual environment, a reality that exists within a third place. Richard was one of these people, and after many months of being killed and always staying the positive and ever helpful explorer who never attacked others, experience finally took its toll upon him.

'One day after another Mage [the highest level mortal character] was butchered by a player killer, something snapped. Thwomp was born, and the darker road of the killer trod. Determined to learn the art of murder, I played yet longer hours – often six hours a night'.

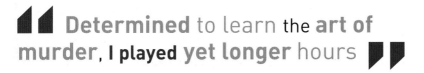

**❮❮ Determined** to learn the **art of murder**, **I played yet longer** hours **❯❯**

An only child of a single parent and with no interest in sport, the role of outsider had perhaps been thrust upon him. Maybe it was inevitable that Richard would become addicted to this world where he could escape completely, where he could find a sense of belonging. 'MUD offered escapism from the banality of my everyday country life'.

Addiction was just around the corner, and with the cost of play working out at 2.5 p per minute, it proved to be as expensive a habit as any drug. When the first £500 telephone bill came through the door, the modem cable was promptly thrown out of the window. 'I was banned but I'd still play. I'd borrow cables from friends or buy new ones. I'd sneak online for a 'quick fix' of tearing around the land. The forbidden fruit tasted sweeter than ever'.

## The MUD Killer

Early on in the life of MUD, killing other players was considered pretty bad form. These fantasy games were largely influenced by the Dungeons & Dragons role-playing genre of the time, and there were strict rules about doing harm to your fellow players as opposed to non-player characters and monsters that formed part of your quest. As time passed, the growing influence of video gaming started to infiltrate the MUD worlds, and 'player-v-player' combat made an appearance. In MUD2 the combat element took on a whole new dynamic: when you were dead, you were dead. There was no respawning of a slain character, no matter how long you had spent nurturing it. Hence the popular saying amongst online world inhabitants at the time, 'You've never lived until you have died in MUD'.

Sometimes Richard would ban himself by deleting the software and destroying any CDs, but within a few days the new CD he inevitably ordered would arrive. And so the addiction was fed, and the murder continued. 'My proficiency rapidly improved, by day I was the sweet guy at school, by night I was a notorious killer'.

> **By day** I was the **sweet guy at school**, by **night** I was a **notorious killer**

### Are You an Online Killer?

The Bartle test (www.guildcafe.com/bartle.php) named after the man who helped create the MUD genre, uses a set of 30 carefully hewn questions to determine your in-game personality. By taking the test you can discover if you are more likely to be an achiever, explorer, socialiser or, for that matter, killer in a virtual environment. Sample questions include 'Would you rather: become a hero faster than your friends or know more secrets' and 'Which is more enjoyable: killing a big monster or bragging about it'. In the interests of research I took the test and discovered I am an AKES personality (Achiever 80%, Killer 73.33%, Explorer 46.67% and Socialiser 0%) which means I like to do well and kill people while exploring on my own.

Over time he discovered the ability to control his addiction to better effect. 'I started just popping into MUD sporadically, sometimes going months without playing'. However, there is one force that remained as strong as ever, and that was the solitary reason Richard was compelled to return to the virtual world, to get back into the game.

That reason was death.

'Chasing someone around virtual mountains, streams and forests has never lost its edge. The buzz is still intense now as it was 10 years ago, the images flicking through my mind, undated. It's like reading your favourite fantasy novel with you both as the hero and the storyteller. Einstein was nearly right. Imagination encircles the (virtual) world'.

Today, more than ever in his life, Richard has started to take control. Two years ago he discovered rock climbing and skiing, real activities to provide the adrenalin rush he used to only experience virtually. 'MUD used to be a time-sink, an escape from the stresses of my life. Maybe I've finally cured my addiction, perhaps you never can – even when you give up the bottle entirely, it's still in control. That's why now I only log into MUD very occasionally. It's an attempt to prove I'm not addicted any more. . . . '

## Virtual Theft, Real Murder

In China a case was reported where a MMORPG player had his priceless 'dragon sabre' sword (well actually it was worth around £400, but had been hard earned through hundreds of hours of online questing) stolen by another player. He reported the theft to the local police who, understandably, explained they could not investigate the virtual theft of a virtual item within a computer game. Perhaps less understandably, the chap then took the law into his own hands and killed the thief in real life.

# 10 Rape of an Avatar

**The first time I encountered** the concept of virtual rape was back in 1993, when the journalist Julian Dibbell published his account of an in-game, text-based attack, 'A Rape in Cyberspace' (www.juliandibbell.com/texts/bungle_vv.html), in the Village Voice. This describes in some considerable detail how a character known as Mr Bungle used a voodoo doll object within LambdaMOO (a text-based online game environment set inside a rambling old mansion) to control other characters and make them perform sex acts. A common immediate reaction is to laugh it off as a prankster with a dodgy sense of humour. In bad taste, certainly, but nothing to be taken too seriously. Yet this was no laughing matter to those people whose characters he abused that night, characters that were more than words on the screen. These were representations of the players, and the abuse left many feeling soiled and dirty.

Fast forward 14 years and the same debate about whether a virtual representation, a collection of computer code displayed upon a screen, can be abused. Whether avatars have rights, moral or judicial. Whether an attack upon a computerised cartoon character constitutes a crime.

Can an avatar be raped?

# Can an **avatar** be **raped**?

Police in Belgium would certainly seem to think so, having investigated the case of an alleged rape of one avatar by another within Second Life. There have even been reports of the Brussels public prosecutor requesting detectives from the Federal Computer Crime Unit to patrol inside Second Life in order to further that investigation.

What isn't clear in this case is the exact nature of the alleged attack. Second Life avatars can, and do, perform sex acts upon one another courtesy of animation add-ons that can be purchased in-world. There is even a 'rape' add-on, but it requires both avatars to consent before it can be activated. Virtual world or not, once consent enters the equation then rape has to leave it. If, on the other hand, what is being referred to here is actually some kind of vocal or textual sexual harassment, while unacceptable (and likely to violate the Second Life terms of service, leaving the perpetrator open to the swift justice of a virtual death sentence), it would again not be rape by most accepted definitions of the term.

Indeed, some argue that if you were to take this to its logical conclusion, then seeing as by definition rape is a forced sexual act and the victim could turn off the computer at any point during any attack, it is hard to see how they would be forced into continuing. So while the avatar itself could, in theory at least, be subject abuse the actual real-life user could not.

Or could they?

Rape is not just about the sexual act, it also very much concerns the domination and objectification of the victim. Psychological scars take the longest to heal, and within such an all-encompassing and immersive environment as Second Life, if your online persona that you have lovingly nurtured is abused, then are you not abused also?

The law is fairly clear-cut when it comes to child pornography, at least as far as the UK is concerned. Section 7 of the Protection of Children Act 1978 defines a pseudo-photograph as being 'an image, whether made by computer graphics or otherwise howsoever, which appears to be a photograph' and goes on to clarify that 'data stored on a computer disc or by any other electronic means which is capable of conversion into a pseudo-photograph' can be used to refer to an indecent image in the eyes of the law. Section 1 of the 1978 Act makes it an offence to make them and distribute, show or advertise them, and the Criminal Justice and Public Order Act 1994 makes it an offence just to possess indecent pseudo-photographs of children.

So while it can be, and often is by those seeking to justify their indulgences, argued that no children were actually hurt by superimposing images of adults and children in a pornographic montage, the result is still illegal. It surely has a bearing on the avatar issue as well, as these are images created by computer graphics that are stored by electronic means and capable of conversion into a pseudo-photograph. In Germany, law enforcement agencies have been looking into cases of alleged simulated sex between adult and child avatars in Second Life, so-called age-play.

If we accept that a line has been crossed when, even in cartoon form, an adult abuses a child in this way then why is it any different for one adult avatar to abuse another?

I would not for a minute argue that a virtual rape is as serious an offence as a physical one, but neither would I dismiss it as a victimless crime. When you remove all the physical properties of a relationship bar the image in front of you, then that image becomes everything, it becomes an embodiment of who you are.

Violate the image, abuse the avatar, and you are also violating its creator. This very real emotional hurt can be seen in all sorts of scenarios in-world, from the ending of a Second Life relationship through to the ending of a World of Warcraft life.

# Violate the image, abuse the avatar, and you are also violating its creator

When it comes to virtual rape the suggestion that the victim could have turned off the computer to prevent it from happening is no different to saying 'she was asking for it' in real life. The notion that all it takes to recover from a virtual sexual attack is to create a new avatar and start again is akin to telling a real-world rape victim to move to another town and get over it.

I doubt that virtual rape will become a real-world crime, outside of violating membership terms and conditions, anytime soon. But then I am not a lawyer.

Vincent Scheurer, on the other hand, is. A qualified barrister who specialises in the law as it relates to the interactive entertainment industry, Vincent set up Sarassin LLP (www.sarassin.net) as a legal consultancy to the video game industry in 2004. 'Essentially, the law of the land will apply to the real world only, not the virtual world – if indeed the law recognises such a thing as a virtual world, which it may not do. So I can't see how pimping or rape can possibly apply to avatars, as they are not human beings; although a simulated rape of an avatar may (depending on the detail) constitute an obscene publication in the real world, which would be illegal.

'Likewise, stealing someone else's magical sword in WoW will not be considered theft of the sword (theft requires the taking of physical property), but might constitute hacking, depending on how the incident occurred. Equally, the "theft" of an item may well constitute a real offence very similar to theft if the item has real world value, or would cost real world money (or goods) to obtain, and has been obtained dishonestly. Quasi-theft offences such as obtaining a pecuniary advantage by deception, or even ordinary fraud, might apply in these cases depending on the precise facts.

'I would argue that there are no virtual actions (or consequences); only real world actions (what a human being does with a mouse and a keyboard) which have real world consequences (changing what someone else reads on a screen), although the conduit between the action and the consequences is the "virtual" world. Real world laws will generally only apply to real world actions which have real world consequences'.

In other words, stealing something online within the context of gameplay in a virtual world is not theft in the eyes of the law. However, it may well be something else. If the item was stolen by someone accessing an account without the owner's permission then it could constitute hacking.

## Linden Lawmaker

Second Life, like other virtual worlds, does have a set of explicit terms and conditions that every resident agrees to when they join. Fall foul of these and you could find yourself banned, your property and possession lost, your virtual identity eliminated. While real-world laws might not apply to your virtual actions, one thing should not be underestimated: within Second Life, its parent company Linden Lab is not only judge and jury but lawmaker as well.

So does the virtual world actually need laws at all, if the crimes that are of any real consequence are already covered by existing legislation? Vincent argues that they absolutely do, if only for sound commercial reasons. 'Clear, fair and impartial laws are a necessary precondition to creating a thriving virtual world. The contrary is rule by dictatorship, where the virtual world provider makes unilateral decisions about the rights of virtual world residents such as reducing inventory, expulsion from the virtual world, without any control. This is pretty much the position with some virtual worlds at the moment, but outside the entertainment sphere it is simply not feasible long term – nobody is going to invest in setting up a business or building an alternative life in a virtual world where he or she could be deleted, or lose all of his or her possessions, at the click of a mouse and without recourse'.

## Defining the Virtual World

'The virtual world provider will usually say that he or she is simply a technology provider or a platform provider, granting users a limited right to use the provider's hardware and bandwidth. This approach, from the outside looking in, is probably legally correct. However, a resident would consider things from a different standpoint altogether, from the inside looking out; and may well consider a virtual world to be absolutely real, comprising a collection of other real people who are real legal entities, and real experiences. Experiences are not easily definable in legal terms, any more than dreams or hopes are, but they are no less real for all that'.
Vincent Scheurer

Alistair Kelman is not so sure. Most famous for being the original computer crime barrister in the UK, successfully defending the earliest cases of hacking to be brought before British courts. In fact, Alistair defended hackers before hacking was even a crime, perhaps most notoriously when Steve Gold and Robert Schifreen managed to compromise the mailbox of HRH Prince Philip back in 1984. It was as a direct result of this case that the Computer Misuse Act eventually became law, making hacking a criminal offence in the UK.

Now concentrating on his role as Head of Content at the Epoq Group Limited (www. epoq.co.uk), Alistair helps produce sophisticated legal technology products for high-street banks and insurance companies. His interest in the legal implications of emerging technologies has never diminished, but he remains sceptical about the need for a rush to legislate against virtual crime. 'I am not too worried about it. We are currently in a development phase where new laws can develop out of reasonable commercial practices and norms. It is a bit like the evolution of mercantile law in Venice in the Renaissance period. During this period merchants and businessmen developed commercial practices concerning the financing of shipping and commerce. Later on the evidence of reliance on these practices led to their being codified into what is now known as mercantile law. The rules of business people became laws. But it did not happen quickly and for very good reasons it is a mistake to legislate too soon. Make the laws too early and they will not correctly map the virtual reality. But as simulations get better and avatars improve there is scope for the development of a system of law in the virtual world'.

Alistair thinks that the digital world in which we live is not yet revolutionary enough to demand new laws. All that could change as we move into a world of 'wet electricity' where technology and biology merge. Don't dismiss this concept as just the ravings of a technology journalist and geek: the process is starting to happen already. The world of pharmaceutical research has created drugs that impact directly upon, and modify, our neurotransmitters. Ever heard of Prozac? In a nutshell it uses this technique to stop serotonin levels from falling too low and so prevents a state of clinical depression. Throw nanotechnology into the mix, the science of very small things indeed, and the area starts to get even more interesting. Research is already underway, for example, to integrate nanodevices with the nervous system in order to create implants that could restore vision to the blind and hearing to the deaf. The University of Nottingham has recently opened a dedicated nanotechnology and nanoscience centre (www.nottingham.ac.uk/nano) and its work in the area of pharmaceutical nanotechnology includes, for example, looking at new ways to deliver drugs into the body.

# The digital world in which we live is not yet revolutionary enough to demand new laws

## Wet Electricity

In his book *Electric Universe*, science writer David Bodanis explores the notion of wet electricity. He looks in-depth at the role played by electricity in what you might think of an inhospitable and sloshing wet human body. How DNA is controlled by potent electrical forces and neurotransmitters determines our very being.

There have been some media-happy academic evangelists prepared to go to extremes, perhaps most famously Kevin Warwick, Professor of Cybernetics at the University of Reading with his 'I Cyborg' project (www.kevinwarwick.com/ICyborg. htm) which saw him implanting a number of small devices connected directly to his nervous system that allowed him to open doors, turn on lights and even 'sense' the love of his wife after she had a similar implant. But while this gives us a fascinating glimpse into the mind of a professor, how many of us would be prepared to do the same? Sure, medical procedures to improve the quality of life are one thing, a mobile phone the size of a microdot in your ear lobe quite another. 'Or the ability to wirelessly search Wikipedia via a brain stem implant which projects a virtual desktop to a heads up display directly into your cerebral cortex?' suggests Alistair. 'What if all your friends were doing this and it was becoming the Facebook for the cyborg generation? These changes **will** be truly revolutionary, and it is then that there must be a legal system to regulate the interface between the virtual world and the real world since most people will be spending their lives inhabiting both and commuting between the two'.

Back in the here and now, Alistair sees the law being tested with cases of virtual copyright infringement for example. There is a case in the United States where a dispute over, of all things, the design of a 'sex bed' for avatars has become the first copyright lawsuit within Second Life. The property concerned, the sex bed, was developed in the real world even when it is only actually used in the virtual world, although a tangible real-world connection might ot ultimately matter.

'The developers of virtual worlds have mirrored the property ownership rules from the real world. This gives rights of ownership and use of assets within the virtual world. All legal systems start with certainty of ownership of property rights and if this is made capricious or unenforceable then the state fails'.

When it comes to the question of avatar rights, in the eyes of the law, then Alistair is quite clear that generally speaking the role of the law is to protect the weakest members of society from coming to harm. 'Currently the virtual world is a long way from the real world in terms of realism and feeling. Real people are unlikely to be harmed by their interaction with others in virtual worlds. When this situation changes then the law will follow. But, no, an avatar does not have any legal rights. However, as your agent its action could be imputed to you.

If someone harmed your avatar, then those actions could be found to have harmed you'.

❚❚ **If someone harmed your avatar**, then those actions could **be found to have** harmed you ❚❚

Real-world laws can apply to virtual actions if there is direct causation, that is, harm in the virtual world can be directly linked to intended harm in the real world. So suppose you have a person who suffers from a medical condition which can cause him to have an epileptic fit if a strobe light is shone in his eyes. When flying through Second Life his avatar gets into a fight with the avatar of someone who knows him and knows of his condition. 'If the enemy avatar has prepared a weapon which shines a strobe light in the face of the avatar, and the real person suffers an epileptic fit, in those circumstances if you could prove that the enemy knew or was reckless as to his actions then liability might be found'.

There are already law firms which have opened up offices within Second Life, virtual spaces where you can meet real lawyers and discuss legal matters that impact upon those living and working within the environment. Unfortunately, until the global community can agree as to what is actually a crime in the real world, then bringing any kind of law and order into the virtual one seems to be lost in the realms of fantasy.

Consider the small matter of jurisdiction.

If I am resident in the UK and publish a website that is hosted on a server in Russia, which in turn publishes something that breaks a law in the USA, where does the liability settle and can anything actually be done to bring me to justice? If I break no laws in the UK where I am based, am I legally responsible for abiding by the unknown laws of another country? Can there ever be such a thing as an Internet jurisdiction in legal terms?

Vincent Scheurer agrees that it is confusing. 'Lawyers and courts have as much difficulty getting to grips with this as ordinary folk. Essentially, courts all over the world find it very hard to give up jurisdiction over someone. So they will usually try to claim jurisdiction if they can, irrespective of where you are based, if there is any connection with their own country. In your example, the courts of the UK, the US and Russia may well all claim to have jurisdiction over your case. The outcome would then boil down to which of those courts could do anything practical about it'.

> ❚❚ Lawyers and **courts** have as **much difficulty** getting to grips **with this** as **ordinary folk** ❚❚

'You are physically located within the UK so the UK courts could deal with you pretty easily. If you have assets in Russia or the US then these could be seized; if you visit there on holiday or on a business trip, they could grab you then. But otherwise it would boil down to extradition: whether there is a treaty between the UK and the relevant country and whether the crime was extraditable'.

And there simply cannot be such a thing as an Internet, virtual, extradition treaty, but only those which exist between real countries and which may apply to online activity such as hacking for example. 'If I commit massive fraud via the internet then I may well be extradited by the UK to any other country whose citizens have been affected by that fraud, provided that the fraud is an extraditable offence and provided that there is an extradition treaty between the two countries. The online or Internet aspect would not be relevant'.

What could be relevant is that unless and until the law catches up with the fast pace of technological change, and that means getting to grips with lives lived and lost in virtual worlds, the opportunity for online vigilante action grows ever stronger. If real-world laws do not apply, the virtual vigilantes will cry 'What is wrong with that?' However, do moral and ethical obligations get removed along with legal ones?

Griefers already cause enough trouble in Second Life, but are generally thought of as being virtual vandals rather than anything more serious. They destroy property, gatecrash public events and generally make a nuisance of themselves. Trapping another resident in a cage or causing flying penises to invade a press conference are just as juvenile and no more harmful than my invading a virtual morris dancing conference 15 years ago and typing 'jingle jangle' for 10 minutes.

When does the juvenile pranking take on a more sinister guise? Is it when a griefer, in the wake of Virginia Tech campus shootings, invades the Second Life University campus and starts shooting at avatars? Or how about when it mimics the real-world structure and aims of a terrorist organisation? Take the Second Life Liberation Army (SLLA), which has been formed as the in-world military wing of a 'national liberation' movement seeking political rights for avatars in Second Life. The SLLA declare that 'as Linden Labs is functioning as an authoritarian government the only appropriate response is to fight. The SLLA will conduct a political and military campaign to ensure its demands are met and avatar rights are established. The SLLA will not seek to harm the normal operation of the world and will only attack agents of the state and other strategically important sites within Second Life'.

▌▌ The **SLLA** will conduct a **political and military campaign** to ensure **its demands are met** and **avatar rights** are **established** ▐▐

Thinking of the SLLA as a terrorist group is perhaps a little misleading. After all there have been no avatar deaths, no great commercial losses inflicted upon Linden Lab by the SLLA. Having avatars taking over the stage at the Second Life version of the World Economic Forum or detonating 'atomic bombs' outside virtual Reebok stores which do little more than produce a startling visual effect are hardly acts of wanton terror.

But Second Life has been exposed to the more serious side of griefing in the past, when a group called the W-Hats literally brought the virtual world to its real-life knees for a while.

Towards the end of October 2005 the group had perfected a method of producing 'code bombs' which, when detonated, simply but awesomely reproduced themselves and flooded that part of the landscape with more code balls. Each newly spawned ball would detonate and create yet more, a perpetual motion that eventually overwhelmed the world, overwhelmed the computer servers upon which the world existed, and caused the entire thing to crash. A single 'attack' would have been bad enough, but multiple bombs were detonated over many days, causing real damage to Second Life because its residents were having trouble logging in. Linden Lab eventually implemented security measures to prevent the problem, but it does show that the potential for virtual acts of terrorism to have a very real-world impact exists. With Second Life users unable to access their world, such downtime can be a costly business.

# 11 The Taboo Busters

**There.com does not allow the** explicitness between avatars as can be found within other worlds such as Second Life. A 'fig-leaf policy' prohibits both nudity and obscenity, so while you might find romance you won't find shops selling interactive genital add-ons or copulating avatar couples. What you will find if you look in the right places within the virtual universe is sex to cater for every fetish.

An interesting thing happens when ordinary people go looking for virtual sex: along with their inhibitions they leave behind any thought of how their in-world actions might rebound into their real lives. They are driven by desire, and the very last thing on their mind is the manner in which they can be traced, or indeed how or who might make use of such information. This is something that a good friend of mine discovered when someone tried to blackmail him after making the connection between his rather well publicized business email address and the very much less-so personal one used for engaging in discussions of sexual nature online. 'When I set up the other identity I didn't give the prospect of a motivated nerd with a grudge a moment's thought'. Not that my friend is easily embarrassed nor ashamed of his sexual preference. He is comfortable with the absolute freedom that a fetish subculture gives him online and off, but like most people he prefers to keep his business and his sex life separate.

# Like most people, he prefers to keep his business and his sex life separate

He continued, 'That and a similar situation with a guy somewhere in New Jersey whose self-esteem was so stupendously low that he would rather be me on line, than himself, have shown me that the traditional script for revealing a hidden identity (loss of status, shame, end of career and so on) actually no longer holds true because everyone's got one. Curiously, the younger nerd generations seem to need to rely on some very old fashioned moral views to justify their collecting and deployment of secret online lives to suit their own ends – everyone else has moved on'.

One thing is for sure, it is becoming ever increasingly difficult to even conceive of such a notion as the virtual world as being some kind of anonymous sexual getaway or a secret second life if you will. 'A new fascism is arising in which MySpace is your confessional and your friends can and will watch and react to everything you do'. Of course 'judged by a jury of your peers' has been a corner-stone of Anglo-Western civilisation for at least the last thousand years, but you can be pretty sure that those who drafted it didn't include the concept that it would apply to that new sweater you just bought, or who you are bonking – or thinking about bonking. 'Every so often' my friend insists 'it is none of the business of the Vicky Pollards of this world as to what I'm going to do or who I am going to see'.

## ❚❚ A new fascism is arising in which MySpace is your confessional ❚❚

Of course, while the social network provides an environment in which the partici-pant feels safe amongst friends and so tends to treat it like a night out with a small group of close confidants, the truth is altogether different. Think of it more as standing upon a stage and baring your soul to an audience that extends even beyond the theatre courtesy of the 'play' being broadcast live on TV. Seen in this light many would, perhaps, choose to reveal less about themselves, or at least think more carefully before opting so to do. The point is, that choice is there to be made: soul-baring confession is not a prerequisite to social networking. How much personal and emotional information you publish is entirely your own decision.

However, while the virtual world continues to provide a perceived safe haven for role playing within the realm of sexual taboo, there will always be the online equivalent of the net curtain twitchers eager to indulge in a little voyeuristic peeping and a lot of malicious gossip, much of it undeserved and more than a touch hypocritical. Is there really a vast amount of moral ground between the married and middle aged man pretending to be a single twenty-something online and the married businessman removing his wedding ring in the hotel bar while away at a conference? Neither is particularly noble behaviour; both are examples of what might be best described as personality fraud. Yet why is the latter pretty much regarded as predictable and accepted, whereas the former is usually considered inherently perverse?

There can be little doubt that people will fall in love in virtual worlds, just as they will in any social space where folk gather. There is more doubt as to whether a purely virtual romance has the potential to last. The relationships that have proved to possess longevity, Heart and Joe, Jo Bleaux and Dweeb, have both involved more than purely in-world virtual contact. Rhonda and Paul, Brian and Sara have all met in the real world.

Despite a whirlwind virtual romance and in-world marriage, Ronnie never actually physically met his bride, and that relationship failed the test of time. I am not suggesting that virtual romance is dead, that a cyberspace relationship is doomed to failure. Far from it, the ability to get to know someone on a spiritual, emotional and intellectual level without the distraction of physical appearance should not be underestimated.

Communication is the key to any lasting relationship, from getting to know a person to getting to keep them. But physical presence plays an equally important role in the relationship dynamic, it fulfils the primitive human need for contact, for physical intimacy with the ones we love.

# You cannot hold the one you love online

While typing '[[Yvonne]]' might let my wife know that I am giving her a virtual hug, she also knows that you can't get the real thing in cyberspace. Even the emergence of 3D graphical worlds cannot change that yet, unless you travel down the fantastical future route of force feedback clothing and electrical impulse generated muscle movements.

Hardly the most romantic of mood setters, I am sure you will agree.

The simple truth is that while you can lose yourself in their virtual eyes, you cannot hold the one you love online.

You can, however, have sex. Cybersex.

I first encountered cybersex some 15 years ago in the earliest of Internet chat rooms. This involved hooking up with someone online, and in effect talking dirty or, more accurately, typing dirty to fuel a masturbatory fantasy. Unfortunately, just knowing that pretty, slim, blonde 18-year-old student called Jenny could actually be a fat, balding, forty-something plumber called Johnny did nothing for my libido. Flirting online was fun, anything more for me was just sad and seedy. I preferred my sexual partners to be in the same room at the same time, to be honest, which is probably why phone sex has never appealed either.

But I am by no means typical, and cybersex has continued to be an online sensation. Now referred to as 'cybering' by those in the know, online sex has moved into the realm of virtual worlds in a big way. There is even one adults-only 3D virtual world that is entirely dedicated to sexual encounter, the aptly named Red Light Center (www.redlightcenter.com).

Describing itself as a 'social experience within a 3D virtual reality space', Red Light Center is an online erotic community which gathers like-minded people within an environment containing virtual nightclubs, hotels, bars and even adult cinemas.

I visited in the cause of research, like any good author would, and can report that it entirely lives up to its name. Whether you are visiting an erotic art gallery, passing through the public sex hall (which is pretty much what you might imagine) or renting a pornographic movie to watch in your web browser, the in-your-face adult theme is unrelenting.

You can head for a hotel, enter a private room and as if by magic talk to whoever you happen to be with using your real voice, rather than typing on screen. Or if your prefer to practise what you preach, then you can actually practise your cybering moves with a 'sex bot' which is fully automated, driven by computer software rather than a human being behind the avatar, to save your embarrassment. Although if you get caught by a loved one practising your sex moves with a computer-controlled cartoon, a red face is probably going to be the least of your worries.

The notion of cheating upon by a partner with a bunch of bits and bytes, canoodling with computer code for want of a better phrase, is likely to impact only upon the shakiest of real-world relationships, to be honest. After all, is it any different from someone masturbating while watching a pornographic movie or reading some steamy work of romantic fiction? Sexual fantasy can, and does, add to the strength of many a relationship and is nothing to be scared of. However, when sexual fantasy becomes virtual fact then the dynamic changes. When instead of interacting sexually with merely a computer-controlled cartoon there is a real person behind the avatar, how different is that to cheating in the real world? The affair between Heart and Joe was never a sexually motivated one in the virtual world, it was more typical of the online world's ability to facilitate a meeting of minds, but would it have made any difference if it were? Rhonda and Paul still fell in love, and there was still a real-world partner who was being 'cheated' upon. A virtual affair has all the odds stacked in favour of the adulterer, at least if the cheated-upon partner is not a member of that same world, has no interest in virtual communities and does not appreciate that real romance and sexual experimentation can be rampant in this make-believe environment. The chances of being caught are minimal if the affair is conducted purely within the virtual realm with no emails, no text messages, no phone calls to be picked up: just that meeting of minds and cartoon bodies in cyberspace.

When it comes to avatar prostitution, things are pretty much as clear-cut. There is always going to be another person involved, although there is the 'which sex' spanner to throw into the works. If the cheated wife were to discover that the virtual prostitute her husband had been meeting online for sexual relief was actually a gay guy getting his kicks and earning a few dollars on the side, would that make matters worse or provide an element of vengeful relief? Although the emotional trauma attached to discovering a partner is using a virtual prostitute is unlikely to be any the less dramatic than if it were a real-world one – they are still paying someone else for sex after all – the physical trauma is certainly reduced. In fact, you could say that the virtual world provides almost a 'green' take on the world's oldest profession. No risk of disease, no risk of physical abuse, no actual contact made. All of which benefit the prostitute as much as the punter.

The mechanics of cybersex are as varied as the real-world equivalent: text-only encounters equate to flirty SMS messages, voice-enabled chat is still just talking dirty on the telephone. When we move into the visual realm the dynamics of the sexual act start to change, however, moving away from any real-world compari-sons. Avatar-driven cybering is most certainly not the same as watching a porn movie, alone or in the company of a partner. In the porn scenario you can only ever be a voyeur, never a participant. As virtual as the environment might be, the emo-tional involvement of participating in an act of avatar sex makes it a very real experience indeed.

Although you can change pretty much every aspect of your avatar appearance just by tweaking at the appearance console, in Second Life your avatar comes sans genitals of any kind, hardly conducive to sexual role play, it has to be said. In order to get these you need to spend a little money, and it can be as little as a pound or so. Go to any of the sex shops in-world and you will find a stall somewhere selling sex accessories, but the daddy of them all is Xcite.

## Getting Xcited

If you want to get your Second Life avatar kitted out with working genitals, sensitive nipples, erotic piercings and the like then you can shop in-world at the Xcite store. A starter kit containing an 'X3 cock' with optional foreskins, a penis that really does become erect when clicked upon, and the control panel to put it to good use will cost a thousand Linden dollars or so. That's a couple of pounds of real money.

Kitted out with the right equipment, it is now possible to remove your avatar clothing and replace it with a broad grin just by touching your balls. Pose balls that is.

## Pose Balls

Pose balls can be found dotted around any adult area of the virtual world. These at first unassuming-looking floating orbs hold a secret that is hinted, rather strongly, at by the label attached to them. These labels will say such things as 'man and woman doggy style' or 'masturbate yourself' or 'female rides male cowgirl fashion' for example. One or more avatars can click on a pose ball to execute a behind-the-screen script, computer code that tells those avatars how to behave by controlling the on-screen animation. That single click on a single pose ball is all it takes to become a sexually active avatar in the virtual world.

## Baby Unicorns

A recent craze within Second Life was to own a cute baby unicorn as a pet. All furry and harmless enough, until you investigate further and discover the only way to acquire one is to have sex with an adult unicorn avatar . . .

Pose balls contain all the code required to animate your avatar, everything from a simple hug or kiss to something more intimate, something more explicit. At the same time, as your avatar is 'receiving oral sex' or 'being spanked' for example, you can be communicating by instant message with the person doing the spanking or performing the fellatio. If you have bought into the clickable body parts fantasy, and equipped your avatar with an erectable penis or stiffening nipples, then it just takes another suitably equipped avatar to 'touch' these to produce the desired effect. The body parts are really nothing more than computer code, but code that can monitor the level of avatar arousal created by that clicking and even enable them to achieve orgasm of sorts.

You don't actually need to have invested in virtual tackle to use a pose ball, but all you get without it is a truly virtual experience with no real interaction, no real involvement. You revert back into the role of voyeur rather than participant. If you want to experience cybering, become part of the sexual dynamic, then you need to immerse yourself fully in the fantasy.

## Webcam Sex

Cybering should not be confused with webcam sex, where consenting adults masturbate in front of each other via video despite being physically remote. Webcam sex uses technology to aid the sexual act, cybering uses technology to create an entirely new erotic genre.

Once kitted out with interactive genitals you just have to find someone who wants to have virtual sex with you. To be honest, this really is not difficult. As long as you are wandering around an openly adult-themed region then chatting to an avatar almost always eventually leads to the question of whether you fancy cybering or

The 'fig-leaf' policy at There.com means people dress up rather than undress, and explicit nudity does not blot the virtual landscape.

not. On the off chance that you cannot get laid even in an entirely virtual sense, this scenario has been catered for. As long as you have some virtual cash you can get a virtual date courtesy of any of the myriad Second Life escort services that exist. The oldest profession has moved into the newest of environments, and by all accounts the avatars that prostitute themselves in this way can make a healthy living, if not a decent one in the moral sense.

# 12 Age Play

**Psychologists have long since leveraged** the use of role play, encouraging patients to find their inner child, regress to a happier time, act out those childhood memories. Lovers have reverted to speaking like toddlers, and using the swings in the play park. Grown men morph into kids every weekend after a few pints at the pub. Age play is an everyday occurrence in the real world and hardly merits a second thought.

Age play in virtual worlds can be a completely different, and highly disturbing, proposition.

There are, undoubtedly, many people for whom the idea of representing themselves with the avatar of a child is purely therapeutic, taking the freedom of a virtual life to encompass a happier time in their real lives. Indeed, within virtual worlds such as Second Life, you will find plenty of dedicated spaces for these avatar children to play. Fun fairs, theme parks, circuses and playgrounds abound. All great places for adults to regress and de-stress.

Yet there is also a dark side to age play. For there are many people for whom it is purely a sexual proposition. For some the virtual world is nothing less than a school for paedophiles.

# For some the **virtual world** is **nothing less** than a **school for paedophiles**

The German authorities have been investgating a case involving the alleged 'pimping' of child avatars providing sexual services to adult characters. The fact that all the people involved will have been over the age of 18 does not dilute the repulsiveness of the virtual act, nor diminish the depravity of those taking part.

No matter how loudly those taking part maintain it is all just a fantasy, no different to role play in the bedroom or dreams in the night, there is no escaping the fact that when stripped back to the naked truth this is, by definition, still a paedophile fantasy.

That same 'no harm done it's only a fantasy' excuse can be found time and time again whenever those involved in virtual age play, predominantly within Second Life simply because it is the virtual environment that has the most creative and technical freedoms, are questioned about their activities. Clubs with names such as Jailbait have provided a focal point for those interested in age play and an environment where all their fantasies can be acted out. Not surprisingly, such clubs are also referred to by the media at large as being nothing more than child sex brothels.

In an interview with the virtual newspaper the *Second Life Herald* (www.secondlifeherald.com/slh/2007/01/ageplay_in_seco.html), Jailbait club manager Emily Semaphore, a 35-year-old librarian in real life but just 13 in Second Life, explains how 50% of the activity in the club is sexual and likens this to people 'playing daddy and his little girl . . . as fantasy roleplay in the bedroom' while dismissing the argument that they must be a paedophile if they are 'being aroused by thoughts or by viewing simulated sexual situations between an adult and child'. She even goes on to accuse those countries where such depictions of paedophile activity, simulated or otherwise, are illegal of penalising people for 'sexual thought crime'.

## Legally Speaking

Although computer-generated imagery depicting children in sexual activity is illegal in the UK, Canada and Italy, the US Supreme Court decided in 2002 that, as no children are harmed in the making of entirely virtual child porn, it should remain legal.

No matter how much they might protest at being labelled as paedophiles, my dictionary defines them as people with a 'sexual attraction to children', and if your avatar is engaged in sexual activity with another that looks like a 10-year-old, that seems open and shut to me. The 'no harm' defence is a red herring, when it comes to *defining* paedophilia, harm is not the issue, the sexual interest is.

I am pretty much as sexually liberated as they come. I have served my time in the fetish clubs of London, indulged in pagan sexual rituals, written a book about sex online and for more than a decade now authored a column for a top-shelf girly magazine. I am most certainly not what you could call a prude in any sense of the word. However, I am a family man. As the father of four kids ranging all the way from single digits to early twenties, my sexual liberation does not stretch to understanding the thought processes of the paedophile.

Although Linden Lab made it clear (blog.secondlife.com/2007/05/09/accusations-regarding-child-pornography-in-second-life) that it has 'absolutely zero tolerance for depictions of child pornography within Second Life' and that 'It goes without saying that anyone engaged in this activity will be permanently banned from Second Life, and subject to legal consequences' age play continues unabated.

## Identity Verification

Second Life operates on an over 18-only policy, with a Teen Second Life world running on a separate 'grid', meaning it's located on different servers and never the twain shall meet. In an effort to ensure that minors cannot access inappropriate content, Linden Lab is introducing a system of identity verification (IDV) using proof of age documentation such as driving licenses or passports, the plan being to only allow these age verified residents access to adult content in mature rated areas in-world.

## Paedophiles Reunited

In July 2007 it was revealed that some 29,000 member profiles had been removed from the US MySpace site, all belonging to convicted sex offenders.

Age play and virtual imagery apart, there can be denying that every innovation that opens up the ability to communicate with strangers also opens the doors for those who would abuse it, and the paedophile is certainly the best example of this breed of technology abuser. But let's not get this out of perspective. Virtual worlds, social networks and the Internet in general are not the real problem here: paedophiles are.

Nobody in their right mind would suggest that DVD players should be banned because child porn is distributed on this medium, or pay-as-you-go (PAYG) mobile phones made illegal because paedophiles use them to groom their victims. So why pick on easy targets such as Second Life, Facebook or any other form of Internet meeting place? Could it be that we live increasingly in an atmosphere of blame, where anyone except ourselves are guilty for our own shortfalls? It is certainly a lot easier to blame the technology that, as far as many parents are concerned at least, is dangerous because they do not understand it and their kids do, than blame ourselves for a lack of parenting skills and good old-fashioned responsibility for the safety of our children.

Predatory paedophiles feed upon this lack of parental responsibility and the lack of meaningful communication within the family. Education is the best weapon we have in the fight to safeguard children online.

That includes understanding the difference between off-line and online paedophile behaviour. Offline paedophiles will typically exist in isolation of one another, for all but the most determined and dangerous the risk of discovery is too great to seek out potentially like-minded souls. Online the landscape is totally different, with communication and networking far more commonplace. The perceived risk of discovery is lowered by an assumption of anonymity, while the more their experiences are discussed with others so the greater the virtual validation of their beliefs. Just like any group with a shared interest, the Internet brings a feeling of belonging, of value and of empowerment. These three attributes applied to a paedophile personality make for a potentially dangerous combination.

Whether by email, instant messaging or a web-based discussion forum, paedophiles are sharing information about the children they have abused or would like to abuse. They are sharing ideas regarding how to use the medium to best effect in a predatory capacity, how to contact, to lure, to groom and to attack. They are also encouraging each other to act out their fantasies, and within the virtual worlds they are doing just that.

## Grooming

A predatory paedophile will groom his chosen victim over a period of time, often many weeks or months, before striking. It might be that they engage with a child on their own level through discussion of music, celebrity, sport and lifestyle by pretending to be of similar age, although usually slightly older to maintain control over the relationship. Others will be clear of their real age and use bribery, both financial and emotional, to show the victim they are wanted. Sex usually does not enter the conversation until quite late into the grooming process, once the trust has already been won, the bonding completed.

## Paedophile Predators

According to former US Attorney General Alberto Gonzales, there are at least 50,000 predatory paedophiles online at any given time, looking for poten-tial victims. The Virtual Global Taskforce (www.virtualglobaltaskforce.com), an international agency comprising police forces across the world working together to combat online child abuse, estimates that one in five young Internet users have received unwanted sexual solicitation, and the number who have been exposed to sexual material on the Internet vary from 25–35%.

Depending upon the age of the victim, sex is usually either introduced through explicit conversation or explicit imagery. It is not too difficult to interest the average teenager in pornography, especially when they are just starting to explore their own sexuality. One particularly insidious method of lowering inhibition is to email photographs of child porn, working on the assumption that showing such sexual imagery reinforces the 'normality' of the act.

When children are shown images of peers engaged in sexual activities, they are led to believe this behaviour is acceptable. This lowers their inhibitions and makes it easier for the molester to take advantage of the child sexually.

## Anti-Grooming Engine

A British company has invented a software application which can spot paedophiles online and catch them in the act of grooming their victims in chat rooms. The Crisp Thinking Anti-Grooming Engine (AGE) (www. protectingeachother.com) identifies the unique 'fingerprint' within a paedophile conversation, based upon a combination of patterns of vocal aggression, sexual comment and solicitations for personal information. AGE gets smarter with every conversation it monitors, and has been tested upon every available grooming conversation transcript from successful US prosecutions to good effect. If a suspect grooming conversation is flagged up, parent and child are alerted simultaneously via SMS text message or email.

You cannot, however, rely on software to police all Internet activity and some basic common sense advice goes a long way in protecting the vulnerable online without destroying the whole social networking and virtual living experience.

## Staying Safe Online

Kids should:

- Only upload images that they would be happy for their grandma to look at. Anything she would find 'too sexy' could encourage sexual attention from paedophiles.
- Keep mobile phone numbers and personal email addresses for real-world friends only. Virtual friends have plenty of communication options and do not need any more.
- Not be loose lipped. Telling friends about a party at the weekend is one thing, telling the world where it is quite another. Real friends can always get in touch for details, but paedophiles will be left home alone.
- Not talk to strangers. A friend of a friend network is one thing, but entering into intimate conversations with a total stranger quite another. The argument is always that it is 'what social networks are for' but my kids should always ask themselves if they would be giving away the same level of personal information to a stranger who approached them on the street and said 'wanna chat?'
- Never arrange to meet with an online-only friend without a parent or other responsible adult in attendance. Images and profiles can be easily faked, predatory paedophiles are experts in grooming potential victims, and there is no way to be 100% sure the 'cool new kid' is not actually something very different indeed.
- Always report incidents online that make them feel uncomfortable, whether through the tone of a conversation, images that are being sent or anything that leaves them feeling vulnerable or scared. Parents, site administrators, chat room moderators and law enforcement schemes such as CEOP and IWF can be thought of as interested parties.

Parents should:

- Site the family computer in a family room, and not allow Internet usage from a computer in a child's bedroom or other 'private' place. Common sense dictates that it is harder for the child to engage in inappropriate activities, and the predator to groom, if an adult can see the screen.
- Use the Internet themselves in order to get a better understanding of how it works, to be able to talk to their children about online risks from a position of knowledge. And also to get involved with the online life of their kids, as spending time online with the kids is no different than spending time playing in terms of relationship building.
  - Supervise Internet usage. Setting time limits on connectivity can prevent addictive behaviour and stop inappropriate relationships from forming. Parents should also be aware of the ease with which mobile phones and next generation games consoles can be used to access the Internet, and monitor this activity as well.
  - Do their homework. A Google search on a child's name or nickname can be very revealing, as can reading their blog if they have one. Such snooping is not the same as reading a private diary, since blogs can be read by anyone online. Parents should make sure they are happy with the level of personal information being revealed.

It is easy to get carried away with the notion that there is a predatory paedophile in every chat room, that they have overrun Second Life in the guise of age-playing avatars, that children are in danger every minute they spend online. But then it is equally as easy to suggest that there is a predatory paedophile on every street corner, posing as vicars in churches and school caretakers, that children are in danger every minute they step out of the front door.

The truth is that the Internet can be a dangerous place to play, but only if you throw your common sense out of the window as soon as the connection is made. Kids must grasp the nettle and realise that virtual life and real life intersect in so many ways.

Adults must adopt a virtual parenting role and talk to their kids about the dangers of online sexual predators in exactly the same way they would warn about never getting in a car or accepting sweets from a stranger.

### Report It

CEOP, the Child Exploitation and Online Protection Centre (www.ceop. gov.uk/reporting_abuse.html), works to tackle child sex abuse wherever it may happen, and that includes the Internet. Affiliated to the Serious Organised Crime Agency, CEOP has a simple online mechanism for reporting any inappropriate or potentially illegal activity with or towards a child on the Internet. If you have need to report inappropriate content, such as child pornography, then you should head over to the Internet Watch Foundation (www.iwf.org.uk) instead.

# IV Logging Off

**Pretty much everything you are**, and everything you have ever been online, is discoverable by anyone with the inclination to go look for it. Your digital footprints are scattered across the Internet, leaving a clicktrail that can be followed whether you like it or not. You can run, but you can never hide from the Google effect. Some people make it easy for the conmen of the new media age to usurp who they are, and the cost of identity theft is measured in more than just financial terms.

**You can run, but you can't hide from who you are online.**

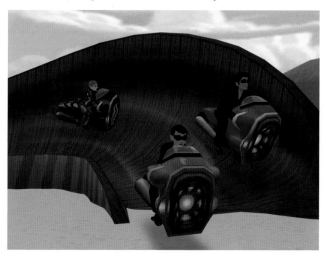

# 13 The Google Effect

**There can be no doubting** that that world changed on 11 September 2001. Perhaps one of the more overlooked consequences has been the erosion of digital privacy thanks to the advancement of electronic eavesdropping techniques and the availability of these technologies to governments around the world in the name of the war against terror.

The investment in data mining is being reaped by both the law enforcement and commercial sectors. Never has it been easier to take little bits of information from multiple and disparate sources, and combine them into an accurate composite portrait of an individual that paints a picture of online habitats and habits alike.

Profiling is, for sure, a highly valuable law enforcement tool that can help spot potential terrorists before they have a chance to act out an atrocity, just as, post-crime, it can help catch a serial rapist or murderer. But profiling can also be used to spot who is most likely to buy which product, where and when. Demographic profiling has been the staple diet of the marketing industry for decades. Perhaps the store loyalty card exemplifies the genre best: in return for the reward of money-off coupons and special member-only promotions, the super-market chain gets access to your retail life within its empire. It not only knows what you spend, but what on and why. It knows what you buy when your usual brand is not available, and how much you are prepared to spend upon every item. Across the course of a year it can build a highly detailed picture of your spending, tailoring promotions to entice you into buying particular products at specific times. Across a volume of customers it can determine the optimum price per item based on the demographic of its customers at any given store, the very reason why prices vary from one outlet to another. Obtain your car insur-ance, mobile phone service and even credit card through the same company and the demographic landscape broadens, the picture getting ever more detailed with every transaction.

Since the Internet has become a staple diet of the public at large, this connected transaction profiling has taken on a whole new lease of life. Substitute your shop-ping list for a list of items you have searched online for, your mobile phone service for your email, credit card for online purchases and car insurance for route plan-ning and it isn't a commercial picture that is painted but a very personal one. Every single time you search for something online, every time you hand over your email address to register at a site, every time you complete a profile at a social network-ing site, every time you post a message within an online forum, every time you do any of these things you are chipping away at your privacy. Little by little you are surrendering data, surrendering detail that can be reformed into the bigger per-sonal picture.

There is a very real phenomenon that has sprung up around this whole Internet privacy issue, widely referred to within the technology community as the Google Effect. This dictates that enough of your online footprint is recorded within the logs of the websites and services you visit to enable anyone with Google access to be able to find out whatever they want about you with a little bit of information retrieval know-how and determination.

Ego surfing is a fun way to discover just what information about you is out there in the blogosphere, and there is even a dedicated tool to let you measure your online ego in the egoSurf search engine (www.egosurf.org) which hunts down the blogs that link to you and where your blog postings rank in various search engines.

## Blogosphere

The blogosphere is the collective name given to the myriad blogs that are published online.

I picked up a few extra points for having an entry in Wikipedia for example, which helped massage my online ego up to a fairly respectable 4890 points. But even this kind of searching does not truly dig down into anything like the amount of data that is stored online, archived within documents and databases that ordinary search engines do not index because they are hidden from the army of software spiders that crawl the Web looking for it. Hidden because the websites themselves are dynamically created on demand, driven by the databases that power them.

This content is collectively referred to as the deep Web and is estimated to be as much as 500 times the size of the World Wide Web that most of us see and the search engines have indexed. Parts of it are searchable through specialist search engines and services, usually expensive subscription-only affairs used within the fields of academia, medicine and publishing. However, that is starting to change, and a new breed of deep-Web search engine is emerging that digs under the surface of the Web for free. Engines such as Wink (www.wink.com) and Pipl (www.pipl.com) search specifically for mentions of your name, or any name you fancy, for example.

# The Deep Web is estimated to be 500 times the size of the world wide web that most of us see

Things are little better offline, where the oft repeated accusation that we are losing our privacy due to some kind of Orwellian 'Big Brother' state-sponsored surveillance program, does perhaps finally have some basis in truth considering the proliferation of CCTV cameras in the Britain.

## Your Digital Footprint

The reality of life online in the twenty-first century is that your digital footprint, a clicktrail of data left behind as you traverse the Web, reveals exactly where you go and what you do. This process has been referred to, somewhat charmingly, as creating digital mouse droppings. Have you ever wondered how that website knows to recommend items based on your previous visit, or a discussion forum can tell which conversational threads you have already read and which are new since your last visit? It is because they keep a log of your activity, or rather you usually keep it for them, on your own computer. Known as cookies, these small data files can be used to personalise a website so that a customised home page is seen by you when you login, or maybe to keep a list of your usual grocery basket at the online supermarket. Or to track which sites you have visited and report back to an advertising agency which can then push specifically targeted adverts in your direction based upon the demographic web profiling it reveals.

According to a report by the Royal Academy of Engineering (www.raeng.org.uk) the UK has more than 4.2 million CCTV surveillance cameras, or one for every 14 people in the country, representing a staggering 20% of the number of cameras worldwide. However, numbers are not the be all and end of this particular argument: truth be told, much of the sacrifice is being made willingly by each and every one of us in our never-ending demand for the convenience and connectivity.

The UK has **more than 4.2 million CCTV surveillance cameras**, or one for every 14 people in the country

Anonymity and privacy, it would seem, are a small price to pay in exchange for immediate access to everything we want. Whatever we do, and whenever we do it, is digitally peeling back yet another layer from the privacy onion. Remove enough layers and, like any onion peeler will confirm, the tears soon start rolling.

So should we be worried? After all, computers are pretty good at this data-filtering malarkey, and if it's helping to provide us with targeted advertising rather than the usual scattergun junk mail, special offers that are relevant and a safer environment to live in, what's the problem? Leaving aside the moral, ethical and political arguments for a moment, one problem is that computers are not as clever as everyone assumes.

In fact, a computer is only as clever as the program it is running, which in turn is only as clever as the person who programmed it. Which is why, when you remove humanity and emotion from the equation entirely, you can end up with conclusions being drawn, connections being made, that seem perfectly sensible in the cold and impassionate computer world of zeros and ones.

Take, for example, the hugely popular TiVo system in the USA. This is a digital television system which operates much like Sky+ in the UK, in that it replaces the video recorder. Whereas Sky+ requires user input to determine what programmes to record, anything from a one-off documentary to an entire sitcom series, TiVo 'learns' from what you watch, and automatically records shows it thinks you will like as well as recommending others it thinks you might enjoy. Trouble is, when people who had watched comedies such as *Will & Grace* or *Ellen* found themselves apparently identified as therefore being gay by their TiVo, which started recording programming geared towards the gay community, unsurprisingly many objected to having their sexual orientation determined, rightly or wrongly, by a souped-up video recorder.

Harmless enough, if annoying to those concerned, the TiVo experience does highlight the dangers of relying upon technology alone to analyse our digital lifestyle and come up with conclusions based upon those online clicktrails and data footprints. If law enforcement agencies were to jump to the wrong conclusion based upon the right data, the consequences could be altogether more serious.

The Google effect, as the name suggests, has nothing to do with recording TV programmes but everything to do with recording your online life. Search engines, and I must stress not Google in isolation, have more in common with an advertising agency than they do a telephone directory.

You use search engines to find information; they use you to generate advertising revenue. Your searches are logged and analysed by powerful computers, and the advertising that gets served up alongside the results of that search will vary from person to person depending upon their individual search demographic: where they are, what they have been searching for, what they are likely to search for. This enables tailored delivery of 'sponsored' search results that are likely to be relevant to you as an individual to be posted. So if you are in London and are searching for tourist attractions, you will see sponsored hits for London tourist attractions and associated services, not a site selling tickets to Disney World or The Louvre.

# You use search engines to find information, they use you to generate advertising revenue

Great, that's a great merging of both content and convenience in a new media duopoly isn't it? Well, yes, but it does have a downside as far as digital detective work is concerned. This information underbelly was well and truly exposed in August 2006 when AOL Research released the raw data from 650,000 searches performed by AOL users over a 3-month period.

Everything had been 'anonymised' in as far as usernames had been removed and replaced with numeric identifiers. Realising its mistake, AOL soon removed the published database – but not before eager privacy activists, and not doubt some with less noble motives, had copied it and posted the duplicate data all over the Web. Just to be helpful, some took that raw data and squirted it into an easy to navigate database with a friendly Web front-end. No harm done though, nobody could be identified from those numeric tags, right?

Wrong!

As any viewer of dodgy US detective dramas over the years will know, it is possible to piece together a very convincing picture from just the smallest fragments of evidence. That is what happened here. By looking at the searches made by an individual numerically tagged user, and doing the lightest of digital detective work, it was possible to produce the name of the person performing the searches.

Probably still no harm done other than a small invasion of privacy, it doesn't matter that we know 'Fred' has been looking for news about the cricket, information on buying a new car and even the slightly embarrassing search for a telephone number to join the Britney Spears Fan Club.

Wrong again.

Here is an actual extract that was compiled just by taking search strings from a single user ID within that AOL search database, the real-world name of the searcher being very obvious but whom I have no compulsion to name here. The point being, would you really want your family, your friends, your employer and in this case your church to know that you had been searching for:

- bank robber hide-outs
- male sissy panty stories
- big bosom mothers
- sissy nightgown training
- tight laced girdles
- Baptist church directory
- old curvy women
- independent Baptist church directory
- Baptist college directory
- adult diaper parties
- husbands that are sissy
- very large bosoms

And perhaps most worryingly of all

- how to make gun silencers

Graham Sadd is a man on a mission, a mission to establish a Personal Identity Exchange (www.paoga.com) to manage the rules of engagement as far as the exchange of personal information online is concerned. 'Context is everything, who I am personally varies depending upon who I am interacting with; my wife, my doctor, my friend, my colleague, the government, a retailer, my employer etc. We are the sum of not only all the things that we have been but also what we want to be. This comprehensive identity is not something that we want to share in total with **any** other individual or organisation. We automatically select what is appropriate to a particular relationship but, when your identity becomes a tradable commodity by third parties, this selection does not take place, let alone any corrections or updates. My identity, whatever that is, is being passed around without my knowledge or permission and, more often than not, to my detriment rather than for my benefit'. A Personal Identity Exchange (PIE) provides the tools by which the individual can record, manage and maintain this comprehensive identity, while only publishing what is relevant and appropriate to any particular relationship or transaction. 'It is the service that Stock Exchanges provide between investors and businesses, that eBay provides between willing buyer and willing seller, that Visa provides between consumer, retailer and banks. Personal Information has become as valuable as our cash and we need to apply the model that the financial institutions have used for years to manage the rules of engagement'.

**❙❙ We are the sum of not only all the things that we have been but also what we want to be ❙❙**

Would you be happy doing your shopping in a town where it was common practise, without your knowledge or your consent, for a sign to be pinned to your back which listed the time and place of your every movement, everywhere you shopped, what books you browsed on the shelf, what items you purchased and how much you paid for them? No, I didn't think so. Yet this is, for all intents and purposes, exactly what happens every time you use the Internet, and very few people are complaining about it. Perhaps it is because we all have an overly inflated expectation of anonymity online? The feeling that because we are alone at the computer, often hundreds if not thousands of miles away from the remote computer we are connected to while shopping, browsing, sending email and so on, reinforces this belief.

Many years ago, when the Web first exploded onto the scene, those of us in the business of advising companies about getting a corporate presence online would use a mantra of 'content is king', meaning that while a flashy presentation is cool and looks good, people will only remember you and keep coming back if there is a compelling content-driven reason for doing so. That has all changed, and while content is still important, we now live in a time where, online and off, convenience has usurped the consumer throne.

We sacrifice our privacy off-line in return for pointless points and we sacrifice our privacy online on the off chance that we might get an email from someone we never even liked that much 10 years ago when we last saw them in the school classroom.

The desire to communicate, to collect friendships, to validate our existence perhaps, has become so strong that few of us can resist the lure of the network.

The **desire to communicate**, to **collect** friendships, to **validate our existence** perhaps, has **become so strong** that **few of us** can **resist the lure** of the network

Unfortunately, in order to participate there has to be a divulging of self, a laying bare of intimate detail, a sacrifice of privacy. Or does there? The answer is yes, but not to the nth degree that so many people take it as they get drawn in, obsessed with the Pokemon-like desire which sees monster trading cards swapped for fleeting friendship, but nonetheless you 'gotta get them all'.

There are a number of ways that you can fully participate in the social experience before you, but without exposing yourself to the same degree of risk as if you rushed in without giving the consequences of your need to connect and communicate any thought at all. Although it might not sound like the ideal way to start a potential friendship, let alone a whole network of them, consider fibbing. Not great big porkers, but subtle little lies that make it much harder for the thief to use your information.

## Sideways Social Thinking

Does it really make that much difference if people think that you were born on the 20th June or the 2nd July? Vary the day or the month, or both, within your date of birth and don't give the real thing out where it is available for public consumption. Same goes with your name, how about inventing a new middle name for yourself? If you have ever fancied being a Brad or Angelina now is your chance. The friends you make will still know you as John Smith, but the would be thief won't get far as John Brad Smith. You can keep in contact with your Facebook friends using one email address, your MySpace pals another and those people you met at Bebo on a third. None of them have to be your main personal account either. The availability and accessibility of totally free-to-use Web-based services such as Google Mail (http://mail.google.com) has made owning truly disposable email addresses a reality.

You can even have Google forward your email to your main mailbox if you like. A side effect is less spam, as Google has impressive spam-filtering capabilities to ensure that very little gets through to bother you. Perhaps the best advice is also the easiest to forget in the heat of the moment, namely to define the limits of what you are prepared to divulge and what should remain between close personal friends only, and then sticking to them. Sit down and make a three-column list: one for the stuff you don't mind sharing with everyone (I like cake, I hate football, cats are better than dogs), one for the stuff that should only be shared with the people you trust in places only they can access it (my daughter is getting married, I am buying a new house, I am starting a new job), and finally one for the stuff that shouldn't be published anywhere (my passport number, my national insurance number, my bank account number.)

When it comes to parental responsibility, short of adopting the kind of 'always there' approach to Internet usage, which is hardly conducive to building the bonds of trust, and notwithstanding the advice dispensed in the previous chapter, the harsh truth is that it is unlikely that anyone will be able to prevent their kids from visiting corners of the Web they would rather remain unvisited. File-sharing sites, illegal music swapping, pornography and anything-goes chat rooms can have an almost magnetic appeal, drawing teenagers unstoppably towards them.

It is **unlikely** that **anyone** will be able to **prevent their kids from visiting** corners of the **web** they would **rather remain unvisited**

Some experts in the field of family computing security have started to suggest that, with regard to protection against identity theft and theft of valuable personal data, the safest form of parental control is to bite the bullet and buy the kids their own computer. Sure, parents must reinforce the responsible Web use message the best they can, let them know that in times of trouble help is on offer as it is with any other rite of passage into adult society. However, preventing kids from using the parental computer at all will protect it against the malware and data security dangers that their usage will almost inevitably attract. Protect their computer with anti-spyware, antivirus and firewall software but be secure in the knowledge that when, not if, it becomes compromised through the installation of a rogue application, the clicking of a bad link or whatever, then the parental data will remain separate and safe.

The separate computer concept also makes post-infection repair a simple matter of reformatting the hard drive and starting from fresh because the worry about restoring all that grown up personal, financial and business data is removed from the equation.

Of course, this does not prevent parents from making childlike mistakes and becoming victims of identity theft with nobody but themselves to blame.

## Malware

Malware is simply the new collective noun for computer viruses, spyware, Trojans and any other software designed to infiltrate or otherwise damage your computer or network. It is, in other words, MALicious softWARE.

# 14 Oh My God, They Stole Kenny!

**Despite what some of the** less informed reaches of the media might suggest to the contrary, identity theft is not a brand new crime that has been born out of the popularity of the Internet. The truth is this particular offence has been around for decades. Con men down the ages have searched through dustbins for bank statements, and corrupt postal workers have stolen credit cards, passports and driving licenses en route to the rightful owner.

Skimming, where credit or bank cards have their details copied by either someone 'double swiping' the card through a second card reader to record the user data or a false front to an ATM machine has been around for more than a decade. However, there is no denying that the Internet has shined a whole new light into the dark art of identity theft, and rocketed it up the crime rankings to the point where it now costs the UK economy an incredible £1.7 billion per year and is the nation's fastest growing crime according to the latest government figures (www.identity-theft.org. uk/faqs.html).

In the USA, the Federal Trade Commission estimates that it takes the average victim of identity theft 175 hours to clear their name and get their identity back, and things are even worse in the UK, where credit scoring company Equifax puts the estimate nearer 300 hours. You might imagine, then, that we would be wary of what information we make available online and to whom. Yet the amount of personal information that we willingly give away to anyone is nothing short of incredible.

During the lead up to the biggest IT security conference last year, researchers from Infosecurity Europe stood outside Victoria railway station in London and simply asked passers by for the kind of information that a would-be thief requires in order to steal your identity, your money and your financial credibility. All those researchers needed was a basic grounding in social skills, a pleasant smile and an air of harmless authority, oh and the promise of a chance to win a chocolate egg.

Every single person asked volunteered their home address including full post-code, 90% added a telephone number, 82% their date of birth and 80% their mother's maiden name, while 86% offered up the name of the family pet. All information that will sound familiar to anyone who has ever needed to confirm their identity with a bank, credit card company or other financial service.

When it comes to social networking sites in particular, in the rush to literally become part of the in-crowd, the connected consciousness of the network age, we tell everyone everything at the drop of a hat. Even the lure of that chocolate egg is not required.

## Identity Theft Defined

Identity theft is, according to the Metropolitan Police definition, the 'unlawful taking of another person's details without their permission. The information stolen can be used to obtain many financial services goods and other forms of identification'. In fact, your personal data can be used to invade both your personal and financial life. Criminals can open bank accounts, apply for credit cards, mortgage property, divert your mail, get social security benefits, rent a flat and more. Career criminals and terrorists alike could be using your identity during the commission of their crimes, leaving the real you exposed to more than just a little embarrassment. Remember Derek Bond, arrested in South Africa and detained for 3 weeks after someone stole his identity and he ended up on the FBI 'Most Wanted' list? Or what about those people caught up in Operation Ore and arrested as suspected paedophiles when their details were used to get credit cards which then paid for access to child porn websites?

Try following your own trail online if you use any of the social networking sites, if you blog, if you participate at all in the Web community. An afternoon is all it will take to convince you that privacy and a desire to be part of the greater global community just don't go together. Everything your mother taught you about not talking to strangers has been forgotten and now we not only talk to them but we actively seek them out and share our deepest thoughts with them.

## Unsocial Networking

According to research by emedia (www.emedia.co.uk) in September 2007, 62% of social network users are worried about the safety of their personal data, and 31% have entered false information in order to protect their identities.

Check out your blog, your MySpace page, your Facebook profile, what you've posted on Friends Reunited and within an hour or two you will be able to put together a pretty precise portrait of your most intimate details: date of birth, family connections, occupation, education, friends' names, interests and hobbies, address, telephone number and so on. Sure, you probably will not have posted all this information in one place, and looked at individually it is distinctly second tier in nature. That is, it is not enough to actually validate your identity on its own. But putting all the pieces of your life jigsaw together is not difficult, and certainly not beyond the ken of the determined thief skilled in the art of social engineering.

Social engineering is simply a term for the collective tricks of the con-man trade used to manipulate people into divulging confidential information, especially within the realm of IT, where fraudster and victim never meet face to face.

Garlik (www.garlik.com), a company specialising in Internet identity issues, called in the help of some of the country's leading criminologists to compile the UK Cybercrime Report in September 2007. This revealed that there were some 3,237,500 cybercrimes committed in the UK during 2006, or, put another way, one every 10 seconds. With 92,000 of those crimes relating to identity theft you would imagine that is about as bad as it could get, but the truth is the actual figure is likely to be much greater. Criminologists tend to agree that around 90% of all cybercrimes actually go unreported. It seems that people tend to think that the police will be either unable or unwilling to get involved, and even that a crime online is not a criminal act in the eyes of the law.

# There were some **3,237,500 cybercrimes committed in the UK** during 2006

According to the Symantec Internet Security Threat Report (www.symantec.com) published in the same month, the value of your identity is probably not as high as you would imagine. There is a black economy that thrives within the darker corners of the Web, the Internet underbelly where cybercriminals trade their ill-gotten gains. The most frequently traded item on this most alarming of black markets are stolen credit card numbers which sell for as little as 25p each when purchased in bundles of 10. Email passwords cost a little more at 50p a time, and the details of someone's bank account a relatively hefty £15. However, if you wanted to buy a stolen identity or at least all the data you would need to 'become' someone else and wreak financial havoc for that real person, it could cost you as little as just £5.

Identity theft pretty much always starts with the same three things: a name, an address and a date of birth. Armed with this information and a forged utility bill or driving license, both of which are readily available on the black market, the thief can apply for a bank account. Given a few other bits of easily obtained, thanks to the Internet, personal information such as employment details, mother's maiden name, and getting a bank account becomes a breeze. It isn't the bank account itself that the thief is interested in, but rather the bank debit card and identity status itself which enables them to acquire dozens of mobile phones before the gig is up. Some will successfully apply for loans, others rent or even buy a car on hire purchase. The fact that it is not the odd lone fraudster chancing his arm, but rather well-organised criminal gangs that are driving the identity theft business is perhaps most worrying of all.

If you want to make life hard for the would-be ID thief, then make sure you do not share the following information with anyone other than the most trusted of online services, and certainly do not place it in the public domain:

- Date of birth (consider changing the month at every non-trusted site you use)
- Mother's maiden name (pets names are also used as a secondary form of login validation after your password)
- National Insurance and passport numbers (very few services outside of government ones actually need to know; travel agents and airlines are the exception for passport data)
- Address and telephone (do not be precise about location, and use a disposable PAYG mobile number if you must)
- Credit card and bank account numbers (never tick the box that says 'keep my details for next time' as there have been numerous cases of databases being hacked and sensitive financial information being stolen)

## Gone Phishing

Phishing, as the name suggests, involves luring an unsuspecting victim with attractive bait. This comes in the form of an email which purports to be from a trustworthy source such as a bank, credit card company or online auction house for example. Social engineering techniques are used to convince the recipient that they need to visit the site, let's say a high-street bank, in order to verify their security details. The link takes them to a convincing copy of the bank website, and prompts them to enter their login and account information. This data is stolen by the thieves, account funds withdrawn and often the identity stolen and sold on as a valuable commodity.

Graham Cluley works for Sophos, one of the world's largest IT security companies, as a Senior Technology Consultant. With more than a decade of experience at the coal face of computer crime fighting, Graham has become one of the world's leading experts on matters malware. A lesser known fact is that he was also the author of the Jacaranda Jim computer game, a virtual adventure created entirely in text, with no graphics at all, back in 1987. But it is his expertise in identity theft that interests me most right now. That and his role in making the small green plastic frog on Facebook such a well-liked personality.

In order to prove a point, that point being we make it all too easy for fraudsters to steal information about us online, Sophos set up an account for Freddi Staur. Yes, it is an anagram of ID Fraudster. Yes, it is a small green plastic frog. Having already established through other research that 41% of people will happily divulge personal information such as email address, date of birth and telephone number to a complete stranger, Sophos wondered if they would do the same for that small green plastic frog.

Freddi himself divulged the bare minimum of personal information about himself, not least because he was a small green plastic frog! Sophos then sent out 200 Facebook friend requests entirely at random in order to observe how many people would respond, and how much personal information could be gleaned from those that did.

**Freddi** himself divulged the **bare minimum** of **personal information** about **himself**, **not least because** he was a **small green plastic frog**

The results were nothing short of staggering:

- 87 of the 200 Facebook users contacted responded to Freddi, with 82 leaking personal information (41% of those approached)
- 72% of respondents divulged one or more email address
- 84% of respondents listed their full date of birth
- 87% of respondents provided details about their education or workplace
- 78% of respondents listed their current address or location
- 23% of respondents listed their current phone number
- 26% of respondents provided their instant messaging screen name

'In the majority of cases, Freddi was able to gain access to respondents' photos of family and friends, information about their likes and dislikes, hobbies, employer details and other personal facts', Graham explains, continuing, 'In addition, many users also disclosed the names of their spouses or partners, several included their complete résumés, while one user even divulged his mother's maiden name, information often requested by websites in order to retrieve account details'.

More often than not, though, it isn't the small green plastic frogs that we have to worry about. Perhaps the most common approach to stealing sensitive information is spyware. And worry people should, because the spyware attacks of today are sophisticated enough that often victims are not aware that they have been attacked until it is too late, until their identity has already been compromised.

## Spyware

Spyware is software installed onto a computer without the owners' knowledge or consent, and with malicious intent. Spyware can monitor keystrokes, steal passwords or open the door to further malware downloads, to name just a few scenarios.

'Written and distributed for illicit financial gain, spyware poses a real and growing threat,' says Graham. 'Web browsing is the most common means of infection. Simply visiting a website can trigger the download of a hidden application onto an endpoint machine. The most common way to attract people to these websites is via spam messages with a link to infected websites. Sophos sees thousands of new infected web pages every day. Spyware is often designed to steal valuable company and personal information. For example, keyloggers record keystrokes in order to capture user ID, password, or bank account information. Browser hijackers redirect users to other websites. Trojans hide other malicious programs'.

## RAT Poison

RATs, or Remote Access Trojans if you prefer, are software applications that infect your computer with a code that, in effect, opens the door to your computer and all its contents to anyone who has the right key. That key will be in the hands of a criminal gang, and not only will they be able to scrape your hard drives of all your personal and financial data, but they will also get to control your PC, zombie fashion, as part of what is known as a botnet. Infected computers are joined together to form a remote-controlled network, a huge resource that is used to send spam, infect other computers and even commit crimes such as denial of service attacks. All the time earning money for the gang, which rents botnets out by the hour, and involving you in a crime you didn't even known you were committing.

While stealing for financial gain is without doubt the most popular reason behind identity theft, with organised gangs being increasingly responsible for concerted and sophisticated attacks, it is not the only reason. 'You may also be interested in stealing an identity if you wanted to cause professional or personal harm to someone who you had a vendetta against,' Graham says. Or perhaps a character within a virtual world or an MMORPG: 'There is malicious software that is designed specifically to steal username and password information from online gamers, giving a third party control of your virtual characters'. A good example was the PrsKey-A spyware worm from 2005, which attempted to steal passwords and user account information from players of the now defunct medieval online fantasy, Pristontale, that at its peak attracted millions of players in South Korea. 'Virtual accessories and powers acquired by your characters can then be sold by cyber-criminals for profit,' Graham explains. 'This kind of attack is particularly prevalent in Chinese-authored malicious code. Indeed in China, over half of all malware written is designed to steal passwords'.

## ❮❮ There is malicious software that is designed specifically to steal username and password information from online gamers ❯❯

A popular misconception is that identity theft is a consumer problem, but in actual fact the corporate world is just as troubled. Because corporate systems in the retail and banking sectors hold vast amounts of financial data on their customers, this information carries a particular premium amongst the cybercriminal gangs. Because the perimeter security around these networks is usually, as you would expect, of a high enough quality to prevent external hacking attacks, the gangs have to look for a way in from inside. During the last couple of years they have been spectacularly successful.

Graham reports that 'TJ Maxx, for instance, had 46 million credit card records stolen. Card Solutions, a payment-processing centre in Atlanta, had 40 million MasterCard credit card numbers stolen, with Visa estimating that 18 million of its customers may have been affected. A man from North Carolina was reported to be facing a maximum possible sentence of 55 years in jail and $2,750,000 in fines if found guilty of illegally accessing the database and downloading contact details of 80,000 members of the American College of Physicians. He then set up a website to sell information about doctors, dentists, lawyers and estate agents to any party prepared to stump up the cash'.

Actually getting realistic statistics on the extent to which identity theft has permeated our culture and society is not easy, even if you are one of the world's leading IT security experts with all the resources of a global IT security company behind you. 'This is not something we track, unfortunately,' Graham concedes, 'and it's likely to be vastly underreported. Remember that identity theft is not like regular theft. In a normal robbery there's a gap on the wall where the Mona Lisa used to hang; not so with identity theft. But we do see more and more malware designed to steal personal information from peoples' computers than ever before'.

## Phish Pharming

Pharming is similar to phishing in motive, but the mechanics are slightly different. Instead of relying upon a victim being fooled by an email into visiting a fake website to capture login and account data, the criminals divert the user when they try to visit the real thing. This is made possible by infecting the victims computer via malware, which often does come courtesy of email, and changing something known as the 'hosts file' which simply redirects all attempts to visit a specific website to another of the criminals' choosing.

As people use the Internet more and more to communicate with friends, family, colleagues and the public it is likely that we will see mischief-makers hijacking online identities to cause problems. The problem with the Internet is that you never know whether you are really speaking to a small plastic frog, Bill Gates, or your next door neighbour. Graham Cluley again: 'We lock the doors to the house when we leave and even ask the neighbours to keep an eye on things when we go on holiday. We spend money on engine immobilisers and alarm systems to prevent our cars from being stolen. We don't wander around with our wallets dangling from our belts, or handbags wide open. So why do we all take so little care when it comes to protecting our most valuable asset of all, our identity?'

At the end of 2006, The Office of Fair Trading (www.oft.gov.uk) revealed that UK consumers are being conned to the tune of £3.5 billion every single year. The detailed analysis suggests that nearly half of the adult population of the UK has been targeted by a scam, and as many as 1 in 15, or 3.2 million people, fall victim to such fraud and lose an average of £850 each. Investment scams were most lucrative with an average pay-off of £5,660 per victim, followed by African 419 advance fee fraud at £5000, property investment scams at £4,240, holiday club schemes at £3,030 and foreign lottery scams at £1,900. The total fraud can be broken down as £1.2 billion to bogus holiday clubs, £490 million in high risk investment fraud, £420 million pyramid-style get-rich-quick schemes and £260 million for lottery scams.

Frighteningly enough, the survey also revealed that a victim has a 30% chance of being scammed again within a year of the first sting, not least because there is evidence that their personal details are included on a 'suckers list' which gets sold between the scammer organisations.

But the biggest shock has to be the fact that only 5% of those scammed actually reported the experience to the police, one can only assume because they felt so stupid at getting conned in the first place.

There are a number of computing common sense steps that can be taken to help prevent you from becoming just another online crime statistic:

- Never provide full security and login information via a link to a website in an email, no matter how believable it sounds or realistic the website looks: reputable organisations will never ask for security information in this way.
- If in any doubt, telephone the organisation (not using a number from the email!) and ask them about if it is legitimate before replying with any personal information at all.
- Never click on links in email messages, but instead type the full address into your browser (or use an existing bookmark) to avoid being tricked into visiting a different site to the one you think you are arriving at.
- Use your common sense. You don't let the 'bloke from the gas board' into your house without ID, you don't accept an obviously fake MOT certificate because the mechanic seemed like a nice chap, so why believe everything an email says and click links blindly?

## Calculating PII

What exactly is Personally Identifying Information (PII)?

- Full name is not PII if both are common, but is if either is uncommon.
- Country, state, city are not PII, but your street address is.
- Age, gender, race are not PII, but a social security or other identifying number is.
- Your salary, job description, workplace are not PII, but your telephone number and email address always are.
- The make of the car you drive isn't PII, but the registration number and your driver's license number are.
- Your bank name is not PII, your credit card number is.

# V  So who ARE we online?

**Having taken the testimony of** people from all walks of life and with myriad different stories to tell, are we any closer to answering the question that started us on this great virtual adventure into the unknown? Is the notion of a single overriding identity a myth? Are we, in fact, the sum of our online parts?

**The search for identity online is no less a mystery than who built the Great Sphinx of Giza.**

# 15 The Collaborative You

**The notion of identity has** changed tremendously during the course of the last 100 years or so. At the start of the twentieth century it was pretty much a given, courtesy of socio-economic pressures, that if you were born of poor parents in a village in Wales then the chances are you would remain there for the rest of your life. Relationships within the family and community would, along with economic circumstances, define your identity. The son of a Welsh slate miner inevitably became a Welsh slate miner himself. There was no chance to break the bonds of identity. Geography, economics and one's place within society formed a fundamental trinity. Post-Second World War things started to change, and relative economic prosperity combined with industrial advancement brought about a much greater freedom of movement, not only geographical movement, but social and economic mobility as well.

The Internet has had the greatest change upon the perception of identity yet. Phrases such as 'shrinking the world' and 'no geographic boundaries' are bandied about and cheapened as a result, but remain vitally important to understanding how the continuity and permanence of our identity, that which is truly us, has been diluted.

The Internet has today become another utility, no different in many ways from electricity, gas, water or even petrol. It is commoditised to the point of just being there to be bought and used without a second thought. As long as the bill is paid at the end of the month, the Internet remains a reality. We use it to do our banking, the weekly supermarket food shop, to keep in touch with friends and family, for education, relaxation and yes, even for work. There is, in fact, only one thing that we do not do online: be ourselves.

## There is, in fact, **only one** thing that **we do not do online**: be **ourselves**

Or do we? Online we are finally freed from the political conventions and cultural restraints that society determines we must apply to everything we do, everything we say, every relationship that we make and break. The fear of making a face to face faux pas, or more correctly the reaction of the other parties and the social, legal and cultural consequences, is removed and by so doing a more honest interaction is ensured. Perhaps then is it more appropriate to think that underneath whatever multiple masks we wear in the virtual world, however many personas we construct, a new collaborative identity is built which ultimately reveals the real us?

In my own case it was not so much a matter of having a split online personality where one persona was totally separate from the other, where there was no control. Instead you can think of my many personalities in terms of clothing, and I was simply trying on as many different styles to see which ones fitted, which suited me the best of all.

Of course, the truth is that there was no 'best fit' as it turned out. I was destined to become the sum of my parts, a composite personality built from the component parts: a little bit from here, a little bit from there. It is a process which continues to this day as I learn from the experiences of my past, and experience the teachings of new worlds and new personalities in the present. I am part dwindera, part Wavey Davey; part hacker, part award-winning IT security journalist; part tattooed punk, part sombre-suited professional. I am a happy geek. Ultimately though the real Davey Winder is none of these things and all of these things simultaneously: **me** is literally all I am.

## ▐▐ I was destined to become the sum of my parts, a composite personality ▐▐

This mix-and-match identity kit was fairly unusual 15 years ago, but today there is a powerful argument to suggest that it has become pretty much the norm. The traditional understanding of identity, which says that we have a single, overriding, core personality that defines us as an individual is just no longer valid as we rush headlong into the digital era. In this age of social networking, blogging, immersive gaming and virtual worlds, there can be no one part of us that reflects all we are. We live in a networked world, an age where everything we do is increasingly connected.

## There can be **no one part** of us that **reflects all we are**

**Create 100 different avatars and there remains a single collaborative you.**

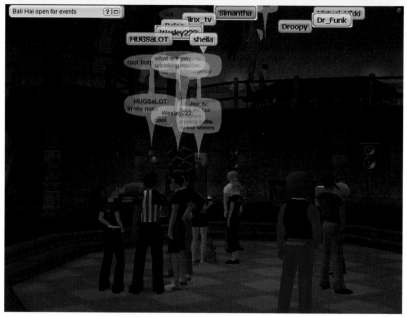

Whereas in the real world there is no escaping from the pretence of identity that we project through the way we dress, the things we say and the way we behave, no matter how much we might compartmentalise depending upon who we are projecting our personality to at any given time, online things are very different indeed. Freed from the restraints of accepted behaviour, fuelled by the perception of anonymity, childlike in our enthusiasm to explore and exploit the brave new world we have discovered, a strange thing happens. Very different aspects of who we are start to emerge: the ruthless killing machine in the multiplayer game, the Lothario in one virtual world and compassionate companion in another, the Facebook social magnet, the forum lurker, the chat room misanthrope, the instant messaging chatterbox.

We might like to think that all of these things are kept separate, that we are still compartmentalising just as we do in life, but online things **are** different. Online there is the Google effect to consider.

Everything we are, everything we do, leaves a digital footprint, a click-trail that can be followed by the search engine software spiders that weave this information into that Web database we all run to when we need to know pretty much anything at all. Unless you have a very common name indeed, it can be something of an eye opener to spend some time literally searching for yourself. When it comes to identity online there can be no doubting that we must move away from thinking of this as painting a portrait of who we are, and instead start considering whether what we actually get is more of a landscape view. Yet even that does not adequately explain the changes that technology brings to this search for self.

Howard Rheingold literally wrote the book when it comes to understanding the dynamic of the virtual community. His seminal tome, *Virtual Communities: Finding Connection in a Computerized World*, may have been published way back in 1994 but remains the nearest thing to a cyber-anthropology bible there is. Indeed, he is credited with inventing the term 'virtual community'.

I'll come clean: my name appears on the acknowledgments page and a few pages are dedicated to my small involvement in helping the cause of UK online community building in the early days, and I value his opinion more than I do most other experts in the field. 'Organizing collective action is inherent in being human. How do you think our skinny primate ancestors, lacking claws, wings, fangs, or the ability to run fast, survived when they moved from the safety of the trees to the predator-rich savannah?' Howard says. 'Collective defence and food-gathering was the form of collaboration that helped Homo sapiens become the biggest predator of them all'. In terms of identity, however, he argues that 'we see ourselves in terms of the groups we belong to'.

## ▐▌ We see **ourselves** in terms of the groups we belong to ▐▌

Yet online culture today is such that we can, and do, belong to so many diverse groups that the small matter of identity must surely be confused rather than clarified by the personalities we choose to display within them. Facebook, MySpace, Second Life, There.com, World of Warcraft are all places where you can yourself the question 'What is one's identity when one is alone?' and come up with a different answer at each. 'They are great playgrounds for experimenting with different facets of one's identity and interacting with people through the masks of fantasy identities, so they are definitely opportunities to exercise identity-play,' says Howard. 'But is one really alone when one knows that so many others are paying attention to what one or one's avatar signals?'

Taking this further, we probably do all display different facets of identity within each online group, protecting perhaps the most fragile of realities underneath it all. However, if we participate in enough of these environments, and given the ever increasing connections between systems and services, is it plausible that we are presenting a collaborative identity that comes closest to revealing the truth, providing the real answer to that question? Howard contemplates for a moment before deciding that 'maybe a single, innermost, true identity is a myth. Maybe identity wants to be more fluid. I do think you are onto something with that 'collaborative identity' theory . . . .'.

> ❚❚ Maybe a **single**, innermost, **true identity is a myth** ❚❚

### Nobody Knows You are a Dog

On the Internet, nobody knows you are a dog. So goes an old online maxim which, to be honest, is only just about managing to hang on to a scrap of validity. Back in the old days of purely text-based virtual communication, it was true, the person behind the account you were conversing with could be absolutely anyone. Apart from perhaps a dog, as they tend not to type that well.

The concept of truly concealing an identity is getting ever more increasingly difficult as the tools to trace and track people online become ever increasingly effective. However, knowing where someone is physically located in the real world, what Internet service provider they are using, and even the real name on the credit card that pays the bills does not equate to full disclosure.

On the Internet, nobody knows you are a dog.

Travel is never tedious in the virtual world.

John Smith, using AOL, based in New York, might publish a blog which says that he is a scientist working in the field of medical research – but how do you know for sure? How do you know if he really does have 20 years of experience working in labs that experiment upon animals as he claims? How can you tell if his conversion to the antivivisection movement as some kind of insider spy is reality or pure fantasy? And perhaps most importantly, does any of it actually matter?

I can answer the last question categorically: yes, it matters.

Being able to filter fact from fiction, wheat from chaff, reality from fantasy will become ever more vital as we turn to the web as some kind of twenty-first century oracle. If we get our world view from the Web, if this becomes the primary source of our political, financial and cultural understanding of the planet on which we live, then we had better be sure of our sources.

News journalism has always been proud of its track record to research the facts, to bring a certain degree of professionalism to the industry, and on the whole it has worked well. Sure, there has been the odd notorious slip along the way, but on balance we know we can trust the serious news media to deliver serious news with minimal spin. Can we truly say the same about citizen journalism? Anyone can start blogging about anything. The previous filtering mechanism of assuming that if a newspaper has published it then it must have some basis in truth has flown out of the window.

There have been many attempts to get around this problem, the most popular being what can loosely be described as the wisdom of crowds. This can be found in places such as Digg (www.digg.com), where readers of news stories vote on the ones that are worthy, and the more votes a story gets then the more exposure it earns and the more people get to read it. The idea being that if a story gets no votes, it gets no exposure, and if a story is over-hyped, then the wisdom of the crowd will vote it down into oblivion.

## Proxy Server

A proxy server simply acts as a bridge between you and the sites and services you connect to online, the end result being that the website sees the proxy server address and not yours.

There is no doubting that this does bring a certain democratisation to the process, but one that is open to abuse. Digg has sophisticated technology that filters out votes that come from the same physical Internet address regardless of how many separate accounts might be hiding behind it, and does the same for those people who would seek to hide that Internet address by using a proxy server. This, though, cannot stop people from grouping together and, in effect, censoring the news by determining what they will vote for and what they will block. Given a big enough crowd playing for the same team, all wisdom could easily be negated.

Perhaps the most famous, or should that be infamous, example of the wisdom of crowds in action can be found in the online encyclopaedia that is Wikipedia (www.wikipedia.com). The principle is simple enough: anyone can write an entry about anything which is then published in the encyclopaedia, but by the same token anyone can edit any entry by anyone else.

The idea being that if an entry is wrong, it will get corrected. If the correction is not accurate, it will get corrected itself. Over a period of time, and given a readership of many millions, the content should end up being factual.

In theory, that is.

In practice the wisdom of crowds does not get everything right, and there have been numerous cases of entries not only being inaccurate, but in some cases potentially libellous, such as when the profile of a retired journalist suggested he was involved in the assassination of John F. Kennedy, for example. While popular entries will, indeed, get amended and corrected through the sheer weight of numbers viewing, entries on niche subjects could go unedited and remain works of fiction for months if not years. Even high-profile entries are not immune: hence the profile of someone such as Tony Blair has been subject to vandalism ranging from adding 'liar' to his political credentials through to revelations of him spilling popcorn on his pyjamas of a night. But there is an additional layer of protection at Wikipedia, in that site administrators have the power to prevent changes to articles and ultimately ban offending contributors from using the site.

Which would be great were it not for the small problem of knowing who these people are, rather than who they say they are. Indeed, one such administrator claiming to be a tenured professor of religion actually turned out to be a college dropout in his early twenties.

The wisdom of crowds is not something that the co-founder of Wikipedia, Larry Sanger, would appear to still have much faith in. His new project, an online encyclopaedia called Citizendium (www.citizendium.org) still allows anyone to author an article for inclusion, but restricts the editing and ultimate publication process to real-world experts in their field, experts with established credentials in the real world.

The Web gives people a platform on which to be published, and has to a large degree replaced the Andy Warhol-inspired TV aspiration of 15 minutes of fame. Replace the time factor with a geographical one and you get the opportunity to appear on the global stage, to conquer the planet no less. Take a look at a random selection of blogs or web home pages and you will almost certainly find a bunch where the author has not got a lot to say but makes the most of the opportunity to be heard by saying it over any number of pages. However, it occurs to me that while the content of those pages can be carefully controlled by the author in order to reveal a certain perspective of personality, the layout of the pages themselves actually says a lot more about the real identity of the writer. It all comes back to visual clues once more, with the format and design reflecting as much about that person as the clothes they wear or the haircut they sport. It isn't foolproof of course, and technical ability plays its part in the end result, but all things being equal the personality of the page will shine through be it neat and formal, artistic and free, edgy and rebellious.

## All things being equal the personality of the page will shine through

The Web of the future is likely to offer an even greater graphical clue to your real identity, and provide the user with a constant visual interpretation of who you are across websites, services and virtual worlds.

**Imagine being able to fly from one virtual world into another with the same avatar.**

Think on this: 60 years ago if you wanted to buy something then you would have to physically visit the seller, exchange cash and leave with the goods. Thirty years ago you could send a cheque by post and have goods selected from a catalogue delivered by mail order. Twenty years ago you could do the same but without posting a cheque, using the telephone and a credit card instead. With the popularisation of the Internet 10 years ago you could order a book or an airline ticket via email or on the web for delivery to the home. Five years ago it became possible to order those same items for delivery online, printing tickets from the web page and downloading electronic versions of book texts. Today you can actually consume certain goods online, buying a ticket to an online concert or an e-book to stock within the library of your house in a virtual world.

The most interesting point to be made here is the speed with which commerce is evolving, and just how quickly we are accepting the move from reality to virtuality. While it took 50 years to move away from a walk to the shops towards a walk to the

## An Avatar for (Virtual) Life

Companies such as Linden Lab, IBM and Google are working towards developing open technical standards to enable the programming of collaborative projects between virtual worlds. Just as there are open standards that allow a document created in one word processor to be opened and worked upon in an entirely different application, so these standards would bring a collaborative dimension not only to the virtual environment but also to the virtual experience. Imagine, if you will, the possibility of creating a truly portable avatar that could travel with you, as you, from Second Life to There.com instead of having a different 'you' in every proprietary virtual space. Imagine being able not only to zoom to anywhere in the planet using Google Earth, and finding yourself standing in an immersive replica cityscape complete with 3D buildings, where you can meet and interact with other virtual travellers. Imagine the Internet not as a network of interconnected networks but a galaxy of interconnected virtual worlds.

computer, it has taken less than a decade to progress from the Internet as a mail order conduit into a purely digital marketplace.

The potential for connecting the disparate locations within cyberspace, the virtual worlds and social networks, the websites and Web 2.0 services such as Google Earth, is nothing less than incredible. The ability to walk an avatar from the social sphere of Second Life into the corporate climate of LinkedIn and have it automatically change clothes from surfer baggies to business suit is not altogether fantastical. All it would take it is a common, standard, accepted

## The Multiverse Network

Some avatar portability already exists thanks to the Multiverse Network (www.multiverse.net), but only if you are travelling between worlds created using its own development tools and using its own specifically tailored web browser to access them. The brainchild of a number of former Netscape developers, the application that first brought a graphical interpretation of the World Wide Web to the masses, the browser and system tools are all available free of charge. Always a good way to encourage the take up of any standard, this free-lunch approach has meant that some 200 worlds are already being built.

language for the computers that create these environments to talk to each other in.

We possess and play many different roles within our life, everything from child to parent, student to employee, friend to lover. However, these roles are played out in a linear fashion, and we have relatively little control over them. Online things are different, very different. We can find a place where every facet of our personality can be explored individually, and simultaneously. This ability to deconstruct the very core of our being is also at the heart of being able to answer the question of who we are online, where our true identity is perhaps revealed once and for all. Think about it: in our everyday life we wear masks that serve to present ourselves in the most suitable light for any given occasion. We tend to act, behave and indeed feel differently when in the workplace, pub, at home, when dealing with the boss, the lover, the children.

## Dissociative Anonymity

Back in 1999, speaking at a press conference while CEO of Sun Microsystems, Scott McNealy responded to a question relating to privacy safeguards in the networking technology being launched with 'you have zero privacy anyway, get over it'. A little under a decade on and perhaps McNealy's Law is at last coming to fruition. We leave a digital fingerprint that can always be traced back to the real world, a clicktrail of routes and destinations that can be read like a map. However, that is not how we perceive the online world, where it is difficult for most users to really know who they are talking to at any given point. This casual anonymity, however misconceived, gives birth to a belief that a virtual character cannot easily be linked to the real life of the person behind it. We separate ourselves from responsibility for our avatar actions, and indulge ourselves in the act of dissociative anonymity whereby online fiction and off-line fact never meet in the middle.

Do any of these masks truly represent what we feel inside? Do they vocalise our deepest thoughts? I would suggest that the answer is no, they do not, not individually nor combined as one. The real us, the person we feel that we truly are, is usually revealed more fully within our dreams and fantasies. Fuelled by the disinhibition effect, which allows us to do and say things online cloaked in the safety net of dissociative anonymity that we would never repeat in the real world, the gates to our inner feelings are unlocked. The hidden aspects of personality bubble to the surface and reveal the person we really want to be, the person we truly are, the person we tend to see when we go online and enter the virtual realm. Surely then, is it not possible that in many ways the virtual self is actually the more honest representation of who we are? Could the answer to the question 'Who are you online?' really be as simple as **the real me** . . .?

# Index